THE CONSTITUTIONAL ODYSSEY OF ARTICLE 370

FROM ACCESSION TO ABROGATION

SUBHRANIL BHOWMIK

Made with ♥ on the Notion Press Platform
www.notionpress.com

Contents

Acknowledgements

The completion of this book, which explores the historical, political, and constitutional trajectory of Article 370 and Jammu and Kashmir, would not have been possible without the profound insights and scholarship of numerous authors and researchers whose works have been foundational to this project.

I am deeply indebted to Dr. Vikas Divyakirti for his comprehensive work, Article 370 & 35-A: Jammu-Kashmir (1947 to 2019), which provided an accessible yet detailed framework for understanding the complexities of J&K's special status. His scholarship has been a guiding force in shaping the narrative of this book.

I extend my gratitude to V.P. Menon for his seminal Integration of the Indian States, an authoritative account of India's post-independence unification that enriched the historical context of J&K's accession. Similarly, M.J. Akbar's Kashmir: Behind the Vale offered a vivid and nuanced portrayal of Kashmir's political and cultural dynamics, which greatly informed the book's historical narrative.

A.G. Noorani's contributions have been invaluable, particularly his books Article 370: A Constitutional History of Jammu and Kashmir and The Kashmir Dispute, 1947–2012, as well as his paper "Article 370: Law and Politics." These works provided meticulous legal and political analyses that underpinned the book's constitutional discussions and diplomatic perspectives.

Ramachandra Guha's India After Gandhi: The History of the World's Largest Democracy offered critical insights into the broader context of India's post-independence challenges, including J&K's integration, enriching the book's historical depth. Prem Shankar Jha's Jammu and Kashmir: The Tide Turns provided a contemporary perspective on J&K's evolving political landscape, particularly during periods of militancy and governance shifts.

I also acknowledge A.S. Dulat and Aditya Sinha's Kashmir: The Vajpayee Years, which offered an insider's view of reconciliation efforts and security dynamics during a pivotal era, adding depth to the book's treatment of the early 2000s.

Finally, I express my gratitude to the readers, whose curiosity about Jammu and Kashmir's place in India's federal story inspires this work. This book is a tribute to the collective pursuit of understanding India's complex and vibrant history.

Prologue

When the British Empire loosened its grip on the Indian subcontinent in 1947, it left behind not just two nations—but a thousand questions. Among them, the most enduring and volatile was the fate of Jammu and Kashmir, a princely state cradled in the Himalayas, divided by geography, religion, ambition, and fear.

This is not just the story of a constitutional provision. It is the story of a fragile moment in time when choices shaped destinies. Of princely rulers torn between power and people. Of leaders like Sardar Vallabhbhai Patel, who stitched the map of India with iron will, and Jawaharlal Nehru, who sought to bind it with idealism and law. It is the story of a war that was never officially declared, of promises made under pressure, of borders drawn not just on land, but on identity.

Article 370 was born out of this crucible—not as a final settlement, but as a constitutional truce. A temporary bridge between the sovereignty of a state and the sovereignty of a nation. For decades, it stood as a legal and political anomaly, fiercely defended, often misunderstood, and always contentious.

This book traces the complex evolution of that clause—from the smoky backrooms of power to the bloodied valleys of Kashmir, from the chambers of the Constituent Assembly to the corridors of the United Nations. It tells a story that begins not with a paragraph in a statute book, but with the shattering of an empire and the struggles of a nation still learning how to breathe free.

To understand Article 370 is not merely to study a law. It is to enter the heart of India's postcolonial journey—its hopes, its contradictions, and its long, unfinished search for unity in diversity.

Message To Readers From The Author

Dear Readers,

This book, a detailed exploration of the historical, political, and constitutional journey of Article 370 and Jammu and Kashmir, is crafted as a single, continuous chapter to preserve the seamless flow of its intricate narrative. This intentional design reflects the complex, interwoven nature of J&K's story within India's broader tapestry—from the tumultuous events surrounding the 1947 accession, through decades of political evolution and conflict, to the transformative abrogation of Article 370 in 2019. By presenting this account without breaks, I aim to immerse you in the unbroken thread of J&K's history, capturing the nuances of its challenges, aspirations, and transformations.

The narrative weaves together the strategic diplomacy of India's post-independence leaders, the legal intricacies of Article 370's provisions, and the socio-political dynamics that shaped J&K's unique status. It delves into pivotal moments—such as the tribal invasion that precipitated J&K's accession, the drafting of Article 370 as a temporary bridge, the erosion of autonomy through political maneuvers, and the bold reconfiguration of J&K into two Union Territories. This single-chapter structure ensures that these events are experienced as part of a cohesive saga, mirroring the persistent and evolving nature of the Kashmir question within India's federal framework.

I invite you to engage deeply with this narrative, which draws on a wealth of scholarly sources to provide a comprehensive and accessible account. This book is not merely a recounting of events but a reflection on the broader themes of unity, diversity, and federalism that define India's journey. Thank you for embarking on this exploration of one of the most significant chapters in India's history, and I hope it sparks curiosity and dialogue about J&K's past, present, and future.

CHAPTER ONE

THE STORY OF ARTICLE 370

The story of Article 370 is deeply rooted in the larger narrative of India's political integration post-independence. To understand the special constitutional status granted to Jammu and Kashmir, one must begin with the events that unfolded during the partition and the formation of the Indian Union.

The process began in 1947, when India was preparing for its independence. The Indian Independence Act was passed by the British Parliament on 18th July 1947, which specified 15th August as the date for the independence of India and Pakistan. India went on to become a sovereign, democratic republic on 26th January 1950 with the commencement of its Constitution.

Before August 1947, the British left the fate of 562 princely states undecided, giving them the option to join either India or Pakistan, or remain independent. Out of these, 549 states chose to accede to India, 10 joined Pakistan, while the status of three states became complicated—Hyderabad, Junagadh, and Jammu & Kashmir.

Role of Sardar Patel and V.P. Menon

Sardar Vallabhbhai Patel was entrusted with the critical task of integrating these states and was required to deploy exceptional diplomatic acumen. Assisting him in this mission was V.P. Menon, who served as the Secretary of the Ministry of States. At the time, Patel held the position of Deputy Prime Minister and headed the Ministry of States (Home Ministry), overseeing political integration and internal security. While Patel provided strong political leadership, Menon played a pivotal bureaucratic role in drafting accession documents and conducting negotiations with the princely rulers.

This background sets the stage for understanding the unique circumstances under which Jammu & Kashmir acceded to India—circumstances that ultimately led to the inclusion of Article 370 in the Indian Constitution.

Patel offered the princely states a straightforward Instrument of Accession, which required them to cede control over three key subjects to the Indian government: Defence, Foreign Affairs, and Communications (including Posts and Telegraphs). Later, Transport was also included under communications, but the three original heads remained central. Interestingly, these were the same areas over which the British government had exercised authority during colonial rule. Under British paramountcy, princely states had internal autonomy but were bound by the Crown in these matters. Patel understood that even after independence, allowing individual states control over such vital domains could lead to fragmentation and jeopardize national unity and security.

He was therefore adamant that the Centre must retain control over these critical sectors to forge a strong and united India. Most rulers accepted this limited surrender of power and signed the Instrument of Accession. While 549 princely states acceded to India peacefully, the process was not entirely without resistance.

For instance:

- Travancore initially declared its intention to remain independent but later changed its stance and acceded in July 1947.
- Bhopal, under its Nawab, also expressed a desire for independence but acceded in May 1949.
- Cochin joined early, and later merged with Travancore to form Travancore-Cochin in 1949.

Thus, while the majority of accessions were peaceful, some required patient negotiation and strategic persuasion.

The matter complicated, as stated earlier, in three key princely states—Junagadh, Hyderabad, and Jammu & Kashmir. These cases did not follow the relatively peaceful path of accession seen with most other states and required special attention from the Indian leadership. Before exploring these complications, it's essential to understand the broader political framework within which India undertook this integration.

A common misconception is that the princely states were automatically handed over to India in 1947. In truth, their integration into the Indian Union began only after independence. Prior to 15 August 1947, India was divided into two political entities: British India and the princely states. While British India—covering about 60% of the territory—was under direct British rule and transitioned smoothly to the Dominion of India, the remaining 40% was made up of over 565 princely states. These states were under British suzerainty, meaning they had internal autonomy but relied on the British for defense, foreign affairs, and communications.

The Indian Independence Act of 1947 marked the end of British paramountcy, rendering the princely states legally sovereign. They were no longer obligated to join India or Pakistan and could even choose to remain independent. This legal vacuum posed a serious threat to the unity of the new nation.

From 15 August 1947 onward, the Indian government, led by Sardar Vallabhbhai Patel and supported by V.P. Menon, initiated the political process of integrating these states. Through the Instrument of Accession, princely states were encouraged to join India by surrendering control only over defence, foreign affairs, and communications—the same areas previously managed by the British—while retaining their internal autonomy. This approach, combining diplomacy, strategic compromise, and in rare cases coercion, ensured the successful unification of India and stands as one of the most remarkable feats of post-colonial state-building.

But Patel's challenge was not limited to princely states alone. Even after independence, some territories remained under foreign colonial rule—Goa, Daman & Diu (under Portuguese control), and Pondicherry, Karikal, Mahe, and Yanam (under French rule). These pockets of non-British colonialism were vestiges of a fragmented pre-independence India, and while their integration would occur over the next decade, Patel's vision and groundwork created the framework for bringing them into the Indian Union. Goa, for example, was liberated in 1961 through military action, while Pondicherry was integrated after prolonged diplomatic negotiations in 1954.

This layered complexity of national integration makes it clear that India's unification was far from automatic—it was a deliberate, nuanced, and multi-pronged process, involving not just political negotiations with Indian princes but also engagements with foreign colonial powers. This backdrop underscores the immense significance of Patel's efforts, as he not only tackled political resistance from within but also had to strategize around external colonial interests and international diplomacy.

Challenges in Princely State Integration

Before delving into the Kashmir issue and the constitutional implications that led to Article 370, it becomes crucial to examine the exceptional cases of princely states that presented immediate and serious challenges—notably Junagadh and Hyderabad. These cases did not conform to the general template of peaceful accession through the Instrument of Accession and, instead, posed existential threats to India's national integrity.

In Junagadh, the ruler Nawab Muhammad Mahabat Khanji III, a Muslim, went against the advice of Lord Mountbatten and signed the Instrument of Accession to Pakistan on 15 September 1947. This decision was highly contentious, as over 80% of Junagadh's population was Hindu, and the state was geographically isolated from Pakistan, being entirely surrounded by Indian territory—except for a tenuous claim of a sea link to Pakistan. The accession was widely seen as unrealistic and provocative, especially since it contradicted the logic of

Jinnah's two-nation theory, which was based on religious majorities. Indian leaders were outraged when Pakistan accepted Junagadh's accession, viewing it as a deliberate attempt to destabilize India's territorial integrity.

Patel took swift action. Citing the principle that the people's will must override the personal wishes of rulers, India responded with administrative control. As public unrest grew and the Nawab fled to Pakistan, the Dewan of Junagadh, Sir Shah Nawaz Bhutto, invited India to take over. A plebiscite was conducted in February 1948, where over 99% of the population voted to join India, legitimizing its integration.

In the case of Hyderabad, the ruler Nizam Mir Osman Ali Khan, one of the wealthiest men of his time and head of the largest princely state in India, declared his intention to remain independent, refusing to accede to either India or Pakistan. This was a bold and controversial decision. Hyderabad, though rich and strategically located in the Deccan plateau at the heart of India, had a majority Hindu population (about 85%), which made the Nizam's stance increasingly untenable in the eyes of the Indian government. To complicate matters further, the Nizam reportedly sought foreign assistance, engaged in clandestine negotiations with Pakistan, and allowed the Razakars—a paramilitary force led by Kasim Razvi—to terrorize dissenters and suppress pro-accession voices.

India, under Patel's leadership, tried prolonged diplomatic negotiations but to no avail. By September 1948, the threat of civil unrest, communal violence, and foreign interference had grown too serious to ignore. Patel finally ordered "Operation Polo", a swift five-day military operation that began on 13 September 1948 and resulted in the annexation of Hyderabad into the Indian Union by

17 September 1948. The operation not only quelled the Razakar rebellion but also showcased India's readiness to use force when national unity and public order were at stake.

These episodes—Junagadh, Hyderabad, and others—highlight Patel's pragmatic leadership, his use of constitutional tools like the Instrument of Accession, and his willingness to act decisively when negotiations failed. His approach laid the foundational precedent for managing more complex and geopolitically sensitive situations such as Jammu & Kashmir, which, unlike Junagadh or Hyderabad, had international ramifications due to its border with Pakistan and China, its geostrategic location in the Himalayas, and its Muslim-majority population under a Hindu ruler.

The Kashmir Conundrum

This brings us to the central issue—Kashmir. While Patel handled most of the princely states, Prime Minister Jawaharlal Nehru took direct charge of Kashmir, partly due to his personal ties to the region and his belief in involving international diplomacy. Lord Mountbatten played a pivotal role during the early days of India's independence, particularly concerning the accession of princely states. As the last British Viceroy and former Supreme Commander of Allied Forces in Southeast Asia during World War II, Mountbatten was acutely aware of the geopolitical sensitivity surrounding the princely states of Junagadh, Hyderabad, Punjab, and Kashmir. He recognized that the partition had created a fragile political climate, and any delay or indecision regarding these territories could lead to major conflict.

In June 1947, Mountbatten visited Maharaja Hari Singh, the ruler of Kashmir, belonging to the Dogra dynasty, at his palace in Srinagar. At the time, Hari Singh was isolated from the prevailing public opinion and seemed unaware of the growing urgency. Mountbatten urged him to make a decision regarding Kashmir's accession to either India or Pakistan before August 1947, cautioning that indecision could lead to serious consequences. He emphasized that although legal independence was technically permissible under the Indian Independence Act, 1947, given the regional volatility and the two-nation theory, remaining independent was practically unrealistic.

Despite this advice, Hari Singh chose not to decide immediately and expressed a desire to keep Kashmir independent. Mountbatten disagreed, stressing the real-world impracticality of such a position, especially as tensions in other princely states were already rising.

Mountbatten also foresaw another issue: the division of the British Indian Army. As British officers were still commanding both Indian and Pakistani forces during the transition, he feared that once full military control passed to the new dominions, unresolved disputes—particularly over strategic territories like Kashmir—could ignite armed conflict. His fears proved prescient.

By October 1947, the situation escalated sharply. Pakistan-backed tribal forces invaded Kashmir, hoping to seize the region by force. This forced Hari Singh to seek immediate military help from India. In return, he signed the Instrument of Accession, officially bringing Jammu & Kashmir into the Indian Union.

This chain of events marked the beginning of the first Indo-Pakistani war (1947–48) and established Kashmir as the central issue in the enduring conflict between the two nations.

The backdrop

As the partition of India unfolded in 1947, the fate of 565 princely states became one of the most urgent and delicate challenges for the new dominions. While most rulers acceded to India or Pakistan based on geographic contiguity and popular will, a few posed exceptional difficulties due to their unique religious, geographic, and political circumstances. Among these, Jammu & Kashmir emerged as the most complex.

The state had a Muslim-majority population (around 77–80%), yet it was ruled by a Hindu king, Maharaja Hari Singh. This religious mismatch bolstered Jinnah's belief that Kashmir had a natural inclination toward Pakistan, especially given the two-nation theory on which Pakistan was founded. On the other hand, India was presenting itself as a secular democracy, where the religion of the ruler or the majority population would not solely determine accession. Thus, Kashmir became not only a territorial dispute but also a symbolic test case for the ideological identities of the two nations.

Meanwhile, discontent was brewing within Kashmir. Sheikh Mohammad Abdullah, a popular Kashmiri leader educated at Aligarh Muslim University, had long opposed the Maharaja's autocratic and discriminatory policies. Although highly educated, Abdullah had been denied government employment by Hari Singh's administration, which heavily favoured Hindus. This discrimination triggered his political awakening and led to the formation of the All Jammu & Kashmir Muslim Conference in 1932, which later evolved into the secular National Conference.

Abdullah, despite being a devout Muslim, rejected the Muslim League's communal ideology, refused to align with Muhammad Ali Jinnah, and instead found ideological camaraderie with Jawaharlal Nehru, a fellow advocate of socialism and secular democracy.

Hari Singh's love for power and his mind-set that he should be king forever significantly complicated the political scenario in Jammu & Kashmir at the time of independence. Despite clear advice from Lord Mountbatten and Indian leadership that the princely states had to accede to either India or Pakistan, Hari Singh remained adamant on preserving his absolute authority. He envisioned an independent Kashmir under his rule, and initially signed standstill agreements with both dominions, hoping to delay any final decision.

However, this indecisiveness came at a cost. India was positioning itself as a democratic and republican country, and in such a framework, there was no possibility for an autocratic ruler like Hari Singh to continue indefinitely as king. On the other hand, Pakistan had declared itself a Muslim country, and given that Kashmir's population was over 77% Muslim, it was ideologically and politically unacceptable for Pakistan to accept a Hindu ruler like Hari Singh continuing in power over a Muslim-majority state. Hari Singh's refusal to democratize governance, his autocratic decision-making, and his failure to engage meaningfully with Kashmiri political voices like Sheikh Abdullah led to growing unrest. Abdullah, supported by the people and ideologically aligned with Nehru, was emerging as the voice of the Kashmiri populace. Yet, Hari Singh had him imprisoned multiple times, fearing his influence. This only widened the legitimacy gap between the monarchy and the people.

Thus, his refusal to democratize and his obsession with retaining personal power isolated him from both the popular sentiment within Kashmir and the evolving political expectations of the subcontinent. This created a complex and fragile situation.

Following the Junagadh incident, where India intervened in a Muslim-ruled princely state with a Hindu majority, Jinnah began to reassess his strategy regarding Kashmir. Observing that Kashmir's population was predominantly Muslim (around 77%), Jinnah believed that if the Hindu ruler, Maharaja Hari Singh, could be removed or discredited, Kashmir could be brought into Pakistan's fold.

After the Junagadh crisis, tensions rise over Kashmir. Pakistan begins exploring options to seize the territory.Discussions began within the Pakistani leadership about action in Kashmir. Jinnah and other officials consider military options but realize direct deployment of regular troops would face resistance. When approached, Gracey (Pakistan's British Commander-in-Chief) refuses to use regular army forces, citing:Uncertainties in logistics and the need for approval from Field Marshal Claude Auchinleck, the British Supreme Commander overseeing military division.Auchinleck had explicitly forbidden unilateral military actions in princely states. Unable to use the regular army, Jinnah authorizes a tribal invasion of Kashmir instead. He believed the Muslim-majority would rise in support of Pakistan. Pashtun tribal forces from the North-West Frontier Province (NWFP) began infiltrating Kashmir with covert support from Pakistan.As the tribal advance continues,the operation turns violent and chaotic. Reports of atrocities cause panic in Kashmir.With tribal forces struggling, Pakistan intensifies the tribal invasion, and some Pakistani military officers accompany the raiders to guide or support them. This was later indirectly acknowledged by Pakistan in UN discussions.

At this point, Hari Singh was still relatively relaxed, believing that his state forces were sufficient to repel any incursion. However, Chief of Military Staff (Commander of the State Forces' frontlines) Brigadier Rajinder Singh was alarmed. He warned the Maharaja that although he had an army, its composition was majority Muslim, and given that Pakistan had declared itself an Islamic state, there was a real risk that the invading force might present the conflict as a religious war. This, he feared, could psychologically influence or even provoke the Muslim soldiers within Hari Singh's own army to either defect or rebel, seeing the attack not merely as a political incursion but as a battle in the name of Islam.

This warning highlighted the deep vulnerabilities within Kashmir's military setup, and as the tribal invasion advanced towards Srinagar, looting and committing atrocities, it became evident that the Maharaja could no longer maintain control on his own.

On 20 October 1947 The tribal militias began their invasion by crossing the border near Muzaffarabad, located about 70 km from Srinagar. Initially, the tribesmen captured Muzaffarabad—a strategically important town on the banks of the Jhelum River. The distance from Muzaffarabad to Srinagar is approximately 70 km, and it was the first step in the tribesmen's push toward the capital city of Kashmir.

On 21 October 1947, After taking Muzaffarabad, the raiders moved swiftly toward Domel and Uri. Domel is around 30 km from Muzaffarabad. By this point, the tribesmen were already halfway toward Baramulla, which is situated approximately 50 km from Srinagar. The road from Muzaffarabad to Uri traverses difficult terrain, and despite the logistical challenges, the tribesmen were able to push forward.

On 22 October 1947, the invaders reached Uri, located about 50 km from Srinagar and near the strategic Uri Bridge that connected the Kashmir Valley to the rest of the region. After taking Uri, the tribesmen advanced toward Garhi and Rampur, both around 60–70 km from Srinagar. These were crucial towns en route to Baramulla. Along their route, the raiders looted villages and created panic, while the state forces struggled to contain the advance.

On 23 October 1947, the Pakistani-backed tribesmen reached Baramulla, which is located approximately 53 km north of Srinagar. Baramulla was a strategic town because it lay on the main road leading directly to Srinagar, the capital of Jammu and Kashmir. The town's capture put Srinagar within easy reach of the invaders.

The raiders spent the next two days in Baramulla, committing widespread atrocities. These included looting, burning, and massacres. Accounts from survivors and reports at the time suggest that sexual violence, including rapes, was part of the brutality carried out by the raiders. These acts were part of the larger campaign of terror aimed at demoralizing the local population and advancing towards Srinagar.

By the time the raiders reached Baramulla, they had already created significant havoc along their path. However, their advance towards Srinagar was temporarily halted as they spent several days in the town, continuing their looting spree. Although Baramulla itself was captured, the situation in the surrounding areas continued to deteriorate, prompting an urgent appeal for help from the

Maharaja of Kashmir, Hari Singh, who sought military intervention from India.

This marked a critical turning point in the conflict, eventually leading to the signing of the Instrument of Accession by Hari Singh on 26 October 1947, thus officially bringing Kashmir into the Indian Union.

Maharaja Hari Singh, who had initially underestimated the threat and remained in Srinagar, fled to Jammu around 23 October. The distance from Srinagar to Jammu is approximately 300 km. Hari Singh was alarmed by the progress of the raiders and the state forces' inability to resist them effectively.

In response to the escalating crisis, V.P. Menon, Secretary of the Ministry of States, flew to Srinagar on 24 October 1947 to assess the situation. He witnessed the chaos and confirmed the urgency of intervention from India.

Following the dramatic escalation of violence in Kashmir, V. P. Menon, the Indian Secretary for States, flew back to Delhi on 24 October 1947. Menon described the widespread atrocities committed by the tribal raiders and the immediate threat they posed to Srinagar, the capital of Kashmir.

Upon his return to Delhi, Menon briefed Lord Mountbatten, Jawaharlal Nehru, and Sardar Patel about the urgency of the matter. Both Nehru and Patel were inclined to act immediately and were ready to send Indian military forces to assist Hari Singh and secure Kashmir. Their support for military action was grounded in the need to stop the tribal invasion and protect Kashmir from falling into Pakistan's control.

However, Lord Mountbatten, despite his close relationship with India's leadership, raised objections to immediate military intervention. Drawing from his experience as the last British Viceroy and his understanding of international diplomacy, Mountbatten cautioned against hasty action.

Mountbatten pointed out that Kashmir's accession to India had not yet been formally completed—Maharaja Hari Singh had not signed the Instrument of Accession at that point. He warned that sending military forces into Kashmir could be viewed as an act of aggression, which could escalate the situation and potentially lead to international complications. Mountbatten emphasized that the region was not officially a part of India yet, and such an intervention could have severe diplomatic consequences.

Mountbatten also highlighted the delicate international situation. He was aware that the United Nations was already taking an interest in the Kashmir issue, and any military intervention could undermine India's position in the UN. He feared that India's premature military involvement might internationalize the conflict, bringing in external powers and further complicating the situation.

India, as a newly independent nation, was still trying to establish its international standing. Mountbatten feared that acting too quickly could damage India's international image and provoke international condemnation. His concern was that an official war with Pakistan, before Kashmir's legal integration into India, could create a diplomatic and military crisis.

Fearing for his life and the collapse of administration, Maharaja Hari Singh left Srinagar and moved to Jammu on 25 October 1947, along with his family and close aides. Jammu, being farther from the advancing tribesmen, was considered safer.

On the morning of 25 October, V. P. Menon, Secretary of the Ministry of States, flew from Delhi to Srinagar in a military aircraft to assess the situation firsthand and consult the Maharaja.

However, by the time Menon arrived, the Maharaja had already left for Jammu. Menon quickly realized the urgency — Srinagar was about to fall. Indian troops could not be sent without formal accession, and time was running out. Menon immediately flew from Srinagar to Jammu to meet Maharaja Hari Singh. In Jammu, he met the distressed ruler, who described the chaotic situation and pleaded for urgent military assistance. This meeting was critical as Hari Singh was now under immense pressure from the tribal forces advancing towards Srinagar.

Hari Singh then contacted the then Prime Minister of Jammu and Kashmir Meher Chand Mahajan, a prominent lawyer and a confidante, who would later serve as a Judge of the Supreme Court of India. Mahajan, along with V. P. Menon, explained the gravity of the situation and urged Hari Singh to sign the Instrument of Accession to India, which would legally integrate Jammu and Kashmir into the Indian Union.

However, Hari Singh was still hesitant. His primary concern was the political and demographic implications of such a decision, given the Muslim-majority population of Kashmir and the potential backlash from Pakistan. He wanted to maintain Kashmir's independence, fearing the consequences of joining either of the two newly created nations, India or Pakistan.

As the situation on the ground grew more dire, Rajinder Singh, a senior officer in the Kashmir State Forces, played a critical role in delaying the Pakistani-backed tribal forces' advance. Recognizing the imminent threat, Maharaja Hari

Singh, then in Srinagar, issued an emergency directive to his Chief of Staff, Brigadier Rajinder Singh, late on 22 October. Singh was ordered to hold the enemy "till the last man and the last bullet" to buy time for political negotiations with Delhi and for potential Indian military assistance.

Responding with remarkable courage and urgency, Brigadier Rajinder Singh mobilized a small force of around 150–260 state troops and rushed to Uri, where the raiders were expected to pass. His troops engaged the vastly outnumbering tribal forces in a series of delaying actions.

On 23–24 October, anticipating the advance of the enemy, Singh ordered the destruction of the Uri bridge, a vital link to Srinagar. This act was critical in halting the raiders' progress and delayed their movement by nearly 48 hours.

Despite fierce resistance, Singh and his men were gradually overpowered. On 26 October, while continuing to fight in the hills near Baramulla, Brigadier Rajinder Singh was mortally wounded and lost his life. His action, however, proved decisive.

This action provided crucial time for the Indian Army to prepare for intervention. The destruction of the Uri bridge by Brigadier Rajinder Singh and his small Dogra force significantly delayed the advance of the Pakistani tribal raiders. These raiders, backed by Pakistan and supported by irregulars from the so-called Azad Kashmir forces, were attempting to seize Srinagar. This delay—at the cost of Rajinder Singh's life—was crucial, as it provided India the time needed to airlift troops to Srinagar on 27 October 1947, following the formal signing of the Instrument of Accession.

On the morning of 26 October, Menon and Mahajan flew back to Delhi to brief the Indian leadership – Nehru, Patel, and Mountbatten – on the gravity of the situation. Mountbatten advised that India could only send troops after receiving a formal Instrument of Accession, to ensure legal legitimacy and avoid international complications.Later that day, Menon returned to Jammu with the Instrument of Accession and presented it to Maharaja Hari Singh. Maharaja Hari Singh signed the Instrument of Accession on the evening of 26 October 1947, legally acceding Jammu and Kashmir to the Indian Union.

There is a widely circulated anecdote (though not officially documented) according to Captain Diwan Singh, the Maharaja's aide-de-camp, Maharaja Hari Singh was deeply distressed by the invasion and the uncertainty of Indian military support. Before going to sleep on the night of October 26, he reportedly told his aide:

"If Indian troops do not land in Srinagar tomorrow, shoot me in my sleep. I do not want to see my people subjugated."

India's Military Response and the Instrument of Accession

Upon Menon's return to Delhi, he immediately briefed Prime Minister Jawaharlal Nehru, Home Minister Sardar Vallabhbhai Patel, and Lord Mountbatten, the last British Viceroy of India, about the situation in Kashmir and the Maharaja's signing of the Instrument of Accession. The document was central to India's legal and political claim over Kashmir, but it still needed the formal endorsement of Mountbatten, the head of state at that time.

Now It was crucial for Mountbatten to sign the Instrument of Accession because, without his signature, the legal framework for India's military intervention in Kashmir could be questioned. The accession had to be seen as legitimate in both domestic and international contexts, especially with the international community closely monitoring the situation.

The signing by Mountbatten occurred on the morning of 27 October and after Mountbatten's signature, the legal process was complete, and India could now send military assistance to Kashmir with full legal authority.

After the signing, there was considerable disagreement about how swiftly India should intervene militarily. Lord Mountbatten, despite his pivotal role in the formal process of accession, was reluctant to send Indian troops into Kashmir immediately. His reservations were rooted in his concerns about international implications, especially the possible escalation of the Kashmir issue into a full-scale war with Pakistan, which could have drawn the attention of the United Nations and jeopardized India's international standing.

Mountbatten expressed that, although the Instrument of Accession had been signed, Indian intervention should be cautious and considered in light of the broader diplomatic landscape. His hesitation was based on the need for diplomatic prudence, fearing that sending in the army too quickly could invite international scrutiny and potentially jeopardize India's fragile post-independence image.

However, Sardar Vallabhbhai Patel was deeply frustrated by this stance. Patel, a staunch nationalist and a more pragmatic leader, was in favor of immediate military intervention. He was keen on defending Kashmir from the Pakistani-backed tribal raiders, who were threatening to overrun the region, and he saw delay as risking the loss of Kashmir to Pakistan. He felt that the situation was urgent and that India could not afford to lose time, especially given that the survival of the newly acceded region depended on swift military action.

The tension reached a peak when Patel, frustrated with the delay, turned directly to the Indian Army Chief, General Sir Roy Bucher, to ask whether the army was in a position to intervene without further delay.

In response, the army cited logistical issues: they claimed a lack of resources and preparation to send troops immediately. The army's logistical challenges were not insignificant, and they made it clear that the situation on the ground was difficult to manage.

But Patel, unyielding in his resolve, insisted that India had no choice but to act decisively. He understood the stakes and was not willing to let Kashmir be lost in the face of international diplomacy. His pressure eventually persuaded Mountbatten to overrule the initial hesitations and approve the military intervention.

In the face of Patel's persistence and the growing urgency of the situation, Mountbatten finally agreed to send the Indian Army to Kashmir. The decision was made that evening, and the first contingent of Indian soldiers, flown in by the Indian Air Force, began arriving in Srinagar on 27 October.

The Indian Air Force played a crucial role in the operation, as it transported troops and supplies to Srinagar, which was already under threat from the advancing raiders. This military intervention, though fraught with political disagreement, became a turning point in the Kashmir conflict, marking the beginning of India's military presence in Kashmir.

As stated earlier in 1946, Sheikh Mohammad Abdullah, leader of the National Conference, launched the "Quit Kashmir" movement against Maharaja Hari Singh's autocratic rule, leading to his imprisonment. Jawaharlal Nehru, a close associate of Abdullah, was deeply concerned about his arrest. In June 1946, Nehru attempted to visit Srinagar to defend Abdullah but was denied entry by the Maharaja's administration and was briefly detained at the border

Jawaharlal Nehru, who had a deep personal and ideological connection with Sheikh Abdullah, pressured Maharaja Hari Singh to release Abdullah, arguing that the popular leader's support would lend legitimacy to India's intervention in Kashmir. Abdullah was released around 25–26 October 1947 and, after the Instrument of Accession was signed on 26 October, the Indian government formally accepted it on 27 October 1947. As stated earlier Indian troops were airlifted to Srinagar on 27 October. Sheikh Abdullah and his National Conference workers actively supported and guided the Indian Army, helping to stabilize the region against the invading forces.

In response to the Indian military intervention and the official accession, Mohammad Ali Jinnah decided to deploy the regular Pakistani Army into Kashmir. However, General Sir Douglas Gracey, the acting Commander-in-Chief of the Pakistan Army (a British officer), refused to comply. He argued that: Pakistan could not engage in war without the approval of the Supreme Commander-in-Chief, Field Marshal Sir Claude Auchinleck.The Instrument of Accession had legally made Kashmir part of India. Direct war would amount to a conflict between India and Pakistan, and since both armies still had British officers, this could potentially lead to a war between British officers on both sides, an unacceptable situation for the British Crown.

Jinnah, having failed to secure military intervention, turned to diplomacy. He contacted Lord Louis Mountbatten, Governor-General of India, and proposed bilateral talks with Nehru to resolve the Kashmir issue. However, Sardar Vallabhbhai Patel objected to this dialogue, stating that:*"The man who sent the raiders is now talking peace. Why should we go to him?"* Nehru, too, became hesitant due to Jinnah's recent public accusations that India had fraudulently taken over Kashmir. These remarks soured the atmosphere and made negotiations difficult.

Despite the opposition, Mountbatten travelled alone to Lahore on 1 November 1947 to meet with Jinnah.During the meeting, Jinnah refused to recognize the Instrument of Accession. He demanded that a plebiscite be conducted in Kashmir to determine its future.Mountbatten insisted that a plebiscite would only be considered after the raiders were withdrawn and normalcy restored.Mountbatten conveyed that India regarded the accession as legally valid, but was open to democratic validation via a UN-supervised plebiscite, after Pakistan withdrew its forces and support to the invaders.

In line with this stance, on 2nd November 1947, Prime Minister Jawaharlal Nehru addressed the nation via All India Radio, making a significant statement regarding the princely state of Jammu and Kashmir. He declared that once law and order had been restored, and the invading tribal forces from Pakistan had been driven out, the future of Kashmir would be decided by its people through a plebiscite, This promise was made following the accession of Jammu and Kashmir to India by Maharaja Hari Singh on 26th October 1947, after Pakistani tribal forces invaded the state.Nehru's commitment to a plebiscite was influenced by multiple factors:

- Political Support from Sheikh Abdullah: At that time, Nehru had considerable confidence in Sheikh Abdullah, the leader of the National Conference and a widely respected figure among the Muslim population of the Kashmir Valley. Abdullah supported Kashmir's accession to India and had a secular, socialist outlook that aligned with Nehru's own ideology.
- Democratic and Humanitarian Principles: Nehru's democratic and socialist beliefs played a crucial role. He feared that forcibly integrating Kashmir into India, especially after just gaining independence from British colonial rule, would contradict the very principles of self-determination and democracy that India stood for. He believed that imposing India's will without the people's consent could foster long-term alienation and resistance.
- International Context: Nehru also made the statement under international pressure and in anticipation of taking the issue to the United Nations, which eventually happened on 1ˢᵗ January 1948 when India formally lodged a complaint against Pakistan's aggression.

However, Nehru's public assurance of a plebiscite created a complex situation. While it was meant to reflect India's confidence and moral high ground, it also internationalized the Kashmir issue. Pakistan used this declaration to argue for a vote, while over time, India moved away from the plebiscite position, citing Pakistan's failure to withdraw its troops from the areas it occupied, which was a precondition for the plebiscite under the UN resolutions.

Meanwhile, the First Indo-Pak War, which had begun with the Pakistani tribal invasion on 22nd October 1947, was still ongoing.

In the face of ongoing conflict and mounting international concern, Prime Minister Jawaharlal Nehru, guided by his belief in international cooperation and peaceful resolution, decided to take the issue to the United Nations. This decision was also influenced by Lord Mountbatten and other advisors who hoped a neutral international body might help resolve the matter without prolonged warfare.

On 31st December 1947, India formally referred the matter to the United Nations Security Council under Article 35 of the UN Charter, which falls within Chapter VI — *Pacific Settlement of Disputes.*

Article 35 allows any UN member state to bring to the attention of the Security Council or General Assembly any dispute that may endanger international peace and security. Chapter VI emphasizes peaceful and non-binding means of conflict resolution, such as negotiation, inquiry, mediation, or recommendations. India specifically chose to file the complaint under Chapter VI, thereby avoiding Chapter VII, which allows the Security Council to impose binding decisions and enforcement actions, including sanctions or military intervention. By invoking Chapter VI, India ensured that any UN action would remain recommendatory, thus preserving Indian sovereignty over Jammu and Kashmir, which had legally acceded to India.In response, the UN passed Security Council Resolution 47 in 21st April 1948. This resolution outlined a three-step plan to resolve the Kashmir conflict:

- Ceasefire:

Both India and Pakistan were to stop hostilities and implement an immediate ceasefire.

- Truce Agreement (Demilitarization):

1. Pakistan was required to withdraw its tribal fighters and nationals from Jammu and Kashmir.
2. India was to reduce its military presence to the minimum necessary for maintaining law and order.

- Plebiscite:

After the ceasefire and withdrawal of forces, a free and impartial plebiscite was to be held under UN supervision to allow the people of Kashmir to decide their political future — either joining India or Pakistan.

Despite the UN's resolution, Pakistan did not comply with the key requirement of withdrawing its forces from Kashmir. Pakistani nationals and tribal fighters remained in the region, and demilitarization did not proceed as planned.As a result, India's military presence remained in Kashmir, as Pakistan did not meet the ceasefire conditions. The plebiscite could not be held due to Pakistan's non-compliance, as the necessary conditions for a free and fair plebiscite were not in place.

Over time, India argued that the situation had changed significantly since 1948, with Pakistan's non-compliance being a key factor. India maintained that the conditions laid out for the plebiscite were no longer feasible due to Pakistan's failure to withdraw its forces and changing ground realities.Consequently, the plebiscite was never held, and the Kashmir issue remained unresolved. It continued to be a territorial dispute between India and

Pakistan, leading to further military confrontations and diplomatic tensions.

In January 1949, both India and Pakistan agreed to a ceasefire, which marked the establishment of the Line of Control (LoC). This line effectively divided Indian-administered Kashmir from Pakistani-administered Kashmir.The LoC was not an official international boundary but rather a military ceasefire line where the fighting had stopped.

It was agreed that the LoC would mark the point where the armies of both sides were situated at the time of the ceasefire in 1949. This line was intended to act as a temporary measure until the situation was resolved through a plebiscite, but the plebiscite was never held.

The ceasefire was brokered by the United Nations and intended to maintain peace, but it also meant that Kashmir was effectively divided into two parts:

- The Indian-administered part (now Jammu and Kashmir).
- The Pakistani-administered part (now Azad Jammu and Kashmir and Gilgit-Baltistan).

The LoC thus became the de facto border between Indian and Pakistani controlled areas of Jammu and Kashmir. Although it was not an official international border, the LoC was meant to prevent further military conflict and provide a line of separation between the two countries' forces.

The LoC became a point of contention for both India and Pakistan in the decades that followed. Despite its establishment in 1949, both countries continued to claim the whole region, leading to multiple conflicts:

- 1965 Indo-Pak War: The LoC was one of the flashpoints of this war, although the fighting mostly took place on the ground, India and Pakistan once again found themselves at odds over Kashmir.
- 1999 Kargil War: The LoC was also a focal point during the Kargil War, where Pakistani forces infiltrated into the Indian side of the LoC, leading to intense fighting before the situation was restored.

The LoC remains in place as the dividing line between the parts of Kashmir controlled by India and Pakistan. However, the situation remains unresolved with both countries continuing to dispute the region.

Despite various peace talks, the LoC continues to be a heavily militarized zone, and skirmishes between Indian and Pakistani forces still occur along the line. The LoC remains a symbol of the ongoing territorial conflict between the two nations over the Kashmir region.

Now, one might wonder why Jawaharlal Nehru sought UN intervention in the Kashmir issue in 1947. After all, India was confident about its position in Jammu and Kashmir, having received the Maharaja's formal Instrument of Accession and already taking military action to defend the region.

The answer lies in a different and often overlooked aspect of India's internal politics and international image — the Hyderabad crisis.

Initially, Nehru had taken a firm stand on not using force against the state of Hyderabad, which had opted to remain independent rather than join either India or Pakistan. Nawab Mir Osman Ali Khan, the Nizam of Hyderabad, had signed a Standstill Agreement with India in November 1947, agreeing to keep the status quo while discussions continued.

However, the Razakars, led by Qasim Razvi, were a radical pro-Pakistan militia group that played a significant role in the conflict surrounding Hyderabad's integration into India. Their primary aim was to annex the princely state of Hyderabad to Pakistan, and they employed violent tactics to further their cause. The Razakars were notorious for their brutal and violent actions, which included widespread communal violence, terrorism, and atrocities. They were responsible for attacking Hindus in Hyderabad, including looting their homes, forcibly converting them to Islam, and committing mass killings. They targeted individuals and families who were perceived as pro-India or who refused to support the Razakars' pro-Pakistan agenda. The Hindus in Hyderabad faced systematic violence, including rape, abduction, and murder. The Razakars used fear and terror as a method of political and religious control. Anyone who was seen as advocating for India's integration or opposing Pakistan's idea of Hyderabad was threatened, tortured, or killed. Public executions of pro-India individuals were common, and mass burnings of Hindu homes occurred as part of the campaign to intimidate and weaken resistance. The Razakars were involved in ethnic cleansing, particularly against non-Muslims, especially the Hindu and Sikh communities. They conducted raids in villages and towns, massacring civilians. They destroyed property and forced people to flee their homes, with large numbers of Hindus being displaced and sent into refugee camps for their safety. The Razakars resisted Indian efforts to integrate Hyderabad into the newly independent Indian Union. They carried out armed rebellions against Indian forces and local authorities. They were supported by the AIMIM (All India Majlis-e-Ittehadul-Muslimeen), which had sympathies with Pakistan's cause. While AIMIM claimed to be non-violent, its leaders and supporters were aligned with the Razakars and their violent methods to achieve their goal of joining Pakistan. The Razakars were known for their use of terror tactics to suppress any opposition. This included the burning of villages, looting, and torturing civilians who were suspected of being against their cause. Religious conversions were also enforced through coercion, and the Razakars sought to eliminate any opposition to their pro-Pakistan ideology through violent means.

The Razakars actively engaged in guerrilla warfare and resisted any attempts by Indian police or the Indian military to restore order in Hyderabad. Their resistance to India's authority further escalated tensions, making it more difficult for the state to function peacefully. Several Indian police officers and local officials who were seen as sympathetic to India were targeted by the Razakars, either through assassination or violent raids on their offices. The Razakars played a significant role in creating unrest in Hyderabad, which eventually led to the need for Indian military intervention. Their actions not only destabilized the region but also led to large-scale violence that could no longer be controlled through diplomacy or political means.

In the face of growing unrest, Nehru was reluctant to take action, as the situation in Kashmir already made India's position complicated, and he didn't want to escalate tensions further on the international stage. Nehru was concerned about India's global image and the potential diplomatic fallout from using force against an independent state like Hyderabad. This concern for India's image and legitimacy in international affairs was a significant factor that pushed Nehru to seek UN intervention in Kashmir.

By doing so, he aimed to show that India was committed to peaceful and lawful methods of conflict resolution. The hope was that this would pre-empt criticism when India would later be forced to act militarily in Hyderabad. Thus, the Hyderabad issue indirectly forced Nehru to take the Kashmir matter to the UN in December 1947 to maintain moral high ground.

However, Sardar Vallabhbhai Patel, India's Home Minister and a pragmatist, was less concerned about international opinion. He believed that Hyderabad, with its instability and growing radicalism, posed a significant internal threat to the newly independent nation. He felt that India could not afford to allow such instability to persist and pushed for military action.

On 13th September 1948, Patel gave the orders for Operation Polo, which was a military campaign to forcibly integrate Hyderabad into India. By 18th September, the operation concluded, and the Nizam's forces, led by Syed Ahmed El Edroos, surrendered, bringing Hyderabad under Indian control.

The Hyderabad issue led to significant international criticism. Pakistan raised the matter at the United Nations, accusing India of violating the sovereignty of Hyderabad. The UN questioned India's military action and whether it was justified, especially since Hyderabad had been a sovereign entity at the time.

Nehru was worried that the military action in Hyderabad could tarnish India's image on the world stage. His concerns grew, especially as Pakistan's foreign minister, Sir Zafrulla Khan, used the military intervention in Hyderabad as a point of argument in international forums. India's use of force could be interpreted as aggressive, which could impact its position in the Kashmir conflict.

While Nehru had hoped to resolve the Kashmir issue internally, the global pressures arising from the Hyderabad operation made him cautious. He sought the UN's mediation to help resolve the issue in a manner that would preserve India's territorial integrity while also maintaining its reputation as a peace-loving nation.

Following the military intervention in Hyderabad and the ensuing violence caused by the Razakars, Nehru was deeply concerned about the scale of the atrocities and the international repercussions. As a response to the violence and chaos, Nehru set up the Sundarlal Commission (also known as the Sundarlal Committee) in 1948 to investigate the human rights violations and atrocities that had taken place during the Hyderabad police action (Operation Polo).

The Sundarlal Commission report, which examined the violence and the aftermath of the Hyderabad operation, stated that between 20,000 to 40,000 people had died during the conflict, with some reports suggesting a higher figure of up to 200,000. The majority of those killed were Hindus, who were targeted by the Razakars and their radical supporters. As discussed above , the Razakars, led by Qasim Razvi, carried out numerous acts of violence, including massacres, forced conversions, and rape, primarily aimed at the Hindu population in the state of Hyderabad. The Sundarlal Commission investigated the scale of this violence, including instances of torture and ethnic cleansing carried out by these extremist groups, often with the tacit support of the Nizam's government.

However, the exact death toll remains a subject of debate. The Sundarlal Commission's estimate of 20,000 to 40,000 deaths is widely accepted, although some sources suggest higher figures. The commission also highlighted the immense displacement caused by the violence and noted the deep scars left on the socio-political fabric of the region.

In the midst of these crises, Nehru began focusing on the Kashmir issue, especially after the Hyderabad operation led to intense international scrutiny of India's actions. Despite Hyderabad being a pragmatic concern for the new nation, the situation in Kashmir was far more complex, and Nehru's diplomatic priorities shifted. After Pakistan raised the issue of Hyderabad in international forums, accusing India of violating the sovereignty of an independent state, the United Nations intervened. This was seen as a potential threat to India's image on the international stage, particularly because India had earlier advocated for the principle of self-determination.

Nehru, already concerned about India's international standing due to the Hyderabad operation, did not want to repeat the same diplomatic blunders in Kashmir. He was acutely aware that the Kashmir conflict had already drawn global attention, and escalating it further would put India in a vulnerable position.

While the Indian military was prepared to take a more aggressive stance in Kashmir, the situation was far more sensitive. Some reports suggest that the Indian Army leaders advised Nehru to give 3-4 months for a military solution to the Kashmir issue, believing that India's superior military position could quickly resolve the situation. However, Nehru was highly reluctant to pursue this course of action. His concerns were rooted in the delicate international situation. He feared that any military escalation could lead to a wider conflict, especially with Pakistan, which could involve other global powers and damage the reputation of a newly independent India.

Nehru's main concern was to avoid the situation in Kashmir turning into an international war. His administration was trying to stabilize the country internally, and he felt that it would be dangerous to further militarize the situation without first attempting diplomatic solutions. Nehru sought to bring the issue before the United Nations to avoid a prolonged military conflict and to present India as a nation that preferred peaceful solutions.

As discussed above ,the UN mediation led to the ceasefire that was implemented in January 1949, which halted the military conflict between India and Pakistan over Kashmir.As a result of this ceasefire, the region was divided into two parts:

- India controlled approximately two-thirds of Kashmir, including the Jammu and Kashmir region and the Ladakh area.
- Pakistan controlled about one-third, which included Azad Kashmir and Gilgit-Baltistan.

The Line of Control (LoC) was established as the de facto boundary between the two territories. This division was intended to be temporary, but it became the permanent military and political boundary between India and Pakistan in Kashmir, leading to decades of tension and conflict.

After the UN-mediated ceasefire between India and Pakistan in January 1949, which established the Line of Control (LoC) and effectively divided Jammu and Kashmir between the two nations, the internal political landscape of Indian-administered Kashmir required urgent attention. The ceasefire did not resolve the issue; it merely paused the military conflict while both nations strengthened their positions diplomatically.

Constitutional Framework: The Genesis of Article 370

Recognizing the need for local governance amid growing instability, the Maharaja of Jammu and Kashmir, Hari Singh, issued a proclamation on 30th October 1947, formally appointing Sheikh Mohammad Abdullah as the Head of the Emergency Administration. This marked the transition of authority from the hereditary monarch to a popularly supported leader, with the backing of the Indian government. Over time, Abdullah emerged as the de facto political authority in Kashmir, while the Maharaja retained nominal power.

In June 1949, a significant political development occurred through the Delhi understanding , an informal understanding between Jawaharlal Nehru, Sardar Vallabhbhai Patel, and Sheikh Abdullah. As per this agreement: It was decided that the constitutional relationship between Jammu and Kashmir and the Indian Union would be defined through the Indian Constituent Assembly. Until the state could convene its own Constituent Assembly, its interests would be represented in the Indian Assembly through nominated members.

Accordingly, four representatives from Jammu and Kashmir were inducted into the Indian Constituent Assembly:

- Sheikh Mohammad Abdullah
- Mirza Afzal Beg
- M.A. Masoodi
- Moti Ram Baigra

These representatives were nominated on a special recommendation from the state's interim administration. Their participation was limited to discussions concerning Jammu and Kashmir, in line with the understanding that the state had acceded only on three subjects: Defence, Foreign Affairs, and Communications.

The Plebiscite Question and the Drafting of Article 370

Now the Instrument of Accession signed in October 1947 was seen as a temporary measure, pending the promised plebiscite to determine the final status of Jammu and Kashmir. However, the plebiscite was contingent upon Pakistan withdrawing all its nationals and tribal forces from the territory it had occupied—something that never happened. Moreover, under UN Resolution 47 (April 1948), the conditions for plebiscite included:

- Withdrawal of Pakistani nationals from Kashmir.
- Gradual reduction of Indian forces to the minimum required for maintaining law and order.
- Holding of a plebiscite under neutral, preferably UN supervision.

Given the complexity of these conditions and Pakistan's refusal to withdraw its forces, the plebiscite remained unimplemented.

Within the Indian Constituent Assembly, it was widely acknowledged that a temporary constitutional arrangement was required for Jammu and Kashmir until the state's own Constituent Assembly could determine its future relationship with India. This led to the drafting of Article

306-A, which would later become Article 370.

Consensus and the Drafting of Article 370

Crucially, the Constituent Assembly followed a policy of discussion rather than voting on most provisions, particularly those involving sensitive political issues. This approach was based on the belief that voting could create divisions and disrupt the spirit of consensus-building necessary for framing a national constitution. In the case of Jammu and Kashmir, voting on its special status could have triggered regional and communal tensions, given the fragile post-partition atmosphere.

Instead, consultation and mutual agreement were prioritized. The drafting of Article 306-A was undertaken with inputs from N. Gopalaswami Ayyangar, a senior administrator and advisor to Nehru, who had also served as the Dewan of Kashmir.When the Constitution of India came into effect on 26 January 1950, Article 306-A was renumbered as Article 370 and included in Part XXI – Temporary, Transitional.

Article 370 thus became the constitutional bridge between Jammu and Kashmir and the Union of India. It codified the temporary and conditional nature of the state's integration, pending final decisions by its own elected Constituent Assembly.

Part XXI and the Inclusion of "Special" Provisions

Now let's understand Article 370 from a technical constitutional perspective — focusing on its placement within the Indian Constitution, its intended temporary nature, and the evolution of related constitutional provisions. Article 370 of the Indian Constitution, which granted temporary special status to the state of Jammu and Kashmir, is placed in Part XXI of the Constitution. This Part, as it stands today, is titled: "Temporary, Transitional and Special Provisions." However, this was not the original title of Part XXI when the Constitution came into effect on 26 January 1950. Initially, it was titled: "Temporary and Transitional Provisions." This naturally leads to a historical and constitutional question: When and why were the words "and Special" added to the title of Part XXI?

To answer this, we must examine the 13th Constitutional Amendment Act, 1962, and its political context, especially concerning the creation of the state of Nagaland. When the Constitution was adopted in 1950, Part XXI included provisions like:

- Article 370 – Temporary provisions for Jammu and Kashmir,
- Articles related to transitional arrangements for the governance of newly independent India.

At this point, the term "Special" was not included in the title because no article under this Part was meant to provide permanent constitutional safeguards — they were either temporary or transitional in nature. However, by the late 1950s, the Naga National Council (NNC) had led a strong movement rejecting Indian sovereignty, resulting in widespread insurgency and demands for secession. To integrate the Naga region peacefully, the Government of India entered into negotiations with moderate Naga leaders, culminating in the 16-Point Agreement between the Naga People's Convention and the Union

Government.As a result: Nagaland was made a full-fledged state on 1 December 1963.

Renaming Part XXI: A Response to Naga Concerns

The 13th Constitutional Amendment Act, 1962 was passed to insert Article 371A into the Constitution, which provided special protections to the state of Nagaland.

Now during the drafting of the 13th Amendment, Naga leaders raised a serious concern:If Article 371A is placed under a part of the Constitution titled "Temporary and Transitional Provisions," how can we be assured that our rights will be protected permanently?

This concern was not raised after the amendment was passed, but during the negotiation and drafting stage itself.The Nagas — still viewing the Indian Union with skepticism — feared that placing Article 371A under a part titled "Temporary" would imply their special rights were also temporary, which could later be revoked by Parliament. Given the region's fragile trust in Delhi, and the violent backdrop of Naga insurgency, this fear carried weight.To address this concern and build trust, the Union Government led by Prime Minister Jawaharlal Nehru ensured that the title of Part XXI was changed at the same time that Article 371A was inserted.

Thus, the 13th Constitutional Amendment Act, 1962 made two simultaneous changes:

- Insertion of Article 371A – giving special protections to Nagaland's social, legal, and customary practices.
- Renaming of Part XXI from:"Temporary and Transitional Provisions"

to "Temporary, Transitional and Special Provisions"

This change was done within the same amendment, to clearly signal that while some articles in Part XXI (like Article 370) were temporary, others (like Article 371A) were special and meant to be permanent.

The amendment explicitly stated:

"In Part XXI of the Constitution, for the words 'Temporary and Transitional Provisions', the words 'Temporary, Transitional and Special Provisions' shall be substituted."

This was not an afterthought or a subsequent amendment — it was a pre-emptive response to a specific political concern raised during the drafting stage, and was included in the original text of the 13th Amendment.

Understanding Article 370(1)(a)

Now, coming back to Article 370, it contains four clauses: 1, 2, 3, and 4. Article 370(1)(a) states that Article 238 shall not apply to the state of Jammu and Kashmir. The exact legislative wording is:

Article 370(1) — *Notwithstanding anything in this Constitution,—*

(a) the provisions of Article 238 shall not apply in relation to the State of Jammu and Kashmir;

To understand the significance of this, we need to look back at the original constitutional categorization of Indian states at the time of the Constitution's commencement in 1950.

When the Constitution of India came into effect on 26 January 1950, the states were classified into four categories: Part A, Part B, Part C, and Part D states. This classification was based largely on the historical legacy and governance structures inherited from British India and the princely states before Independence.

Classification of States in 1950

- Part A States

1. Origin: These were the former Governor's provinces of British India, directly governed by the British before Independence.
2. Governance: These states were administered by a Governor appointed by the President of India, and had their own elected state legislatures.
3. Legal Provisions: Part A states were governed under Part VI of the Constitution (Articles 152 to 237).
4. Examples: Bombay, Madras, Assam, Bihar, Madhya Pradesh (formerly Central Provinces and Berar), Punjab (formerly East Punjab), Uttar Pradesh (formerly United Provinces), Orissa, and West Bengal.

- Part B States

1. Origin: These were former princely states or groups of princely states that had acceded to India after Independence.
2. Governance: These states were governed by a Rajpramukh—a constitutional head who was usually the former ruler of the largest princely state in the union or a nominated person. The Rajpramukh was appointed by the President of India and worked alongside an elected state legislature.

3. Legal Provisions: Part B states were governed under Part 7 of the Constitution (under Article 238).
4. Examples: Hyderabad, Jammu and Kashmir, Mysore, Rajasthan, Patiala and East Punjab States Union (PEPSU), Madhya Bharat, Saurashtra, and Travancore-Cochin.

- Part C States

1. Origin: These states comprised both former Chief Commissioners' provinces and some smaller princely states.
2. Governance: They were administered by a Chief Commissioner appointed by the President of India, without an elected legislature initially (though some later got legislative assemblies).
3. Legal Provisions: Part C states were governed under Part VIII of the Constitution (Articles 239 to 242).
4. Examples: Delhi, Himachal Pradesh, Ajmer, Bhopal, Bilaspur, Coorg, Manipur, Tripura, and Vindhya Pradesh.

- Part D State

1. Origin: This category consisted of a single territory.
2. Governance: Administered by a Lieutenant Governor appointed by the central government.
3. Legal Provisions: The Andaman and Nicobar Islands were governed under Part IX of the Constitution (Article 243).

.

.

Special Status of Part B States and Jammu and Kashmir

Part B states were primarily former princely states or groups of princely states that had acceded to the Indian Union after Independence in 1947. These states had enjoyed varying degrees of autonomy under British suzerainty, ruled by hereditary monarchs.Unlike Part A states, which were former British provinces directly governed by Governors, Part B states retained significant privileges to acknowledge their rulers' status and to ensure smooth integration into the Indian Union.The Government of India, especially under the leadership of Sardar Vallabhbhai Patel, allowed the rulers of these princely states to retain their titles and constitutional status as Rajpramukh (constitutional head of the state). The Rajpramukh was appointed by the President of India, usually the former ruler of the largest princely state in the union or a nominated person.To compensate the former rulers for surrendering their sovereignty, the Indian government granted a Privy Purse—an annual payment (effectively a pension)—which assured them a dignified lifestyle post-integration.

This was a key incentive to encourage their peaceful accession to India. It is often noted in historical records that some princely states had their own armies before accession, but after integration into India, the standing armies of princely states were merged into the Indian Army. The special arrangement allowed these states temporary retention of forces until full integration; however, no princely state retained an independent army permanently after 1948.

Article 370(1)(a) and Jammu and Kashmir's Distinct Status

Now coming to discussion again when Article 370(1)(a) stated that the provisions of Article 238 shall not apply in relation to the State of Jammu and Kashmir. This legislative wording effectively positioned Jammu and Kashmir differently from other states, particularly Part B states, which were governed under Article 238.By excluding Article 238, Jammu and Kashmir retained a distinct constitutional status, giving it more autonomy than even the Part B states, which were former princely states with special arrangements under Article 238. In this sense, Jammu and Kashmir enjoyed a higher level of self-governance compared to the Part B category.

Reorganization of States and Legal Implications

Now in 1956, the Seventh Amendment of the Constitution of India was enacted as part of the States Reorganisation Act. This amendment reorganized the boundaries and classifications of Indian states on linguistic and administrative lines. The classification of states into Parts A, B, C, and D was abolished and was replaced with a simpler structure dividing the country into States and Union Territories.

The deletion of Article 238 and the reorganization of states meant that the special provisions that applied to Part B states were subsumed under a new constitutional framework. Since Article 370(1)(a) specifically excludes the application of Article 238 to Jammu and Kashmir, the deletion of Article 238 made this clause technically redundant or "meaningless" from a strictly legal standpoint. The constitutional framework today recognizes States and Union Territories under two separate lists in the Seventh Schedule, removing the earlier categories (Part A, B, C, D) entirely.

Although the deletion of Article 238 in 1956 made Article 370(1)(a) technically redundant, Article 370 as a whole remained central to the constitutional relationship between Jammu and Kashmir and the Union of India. It served as the legal bridge that connected the unique terms of accession to the evolving framework of the Indian Constitution. More importantly, Article 370 was the mechanism through which constitutional provisions and parliamentary laws could be extended to Jammu and Kashmir, but only under specific conditions.

Legislative Powers Under Article 370(1)(b)

Under Article 370(1)(b), the power of the Indian Parliament to legislate for Jammu and Kashmir was explicitly limited. This clause laid down a two-fold structure:

- Clause (i) permitted Parliament to legislate on those matters in the Union List and Concurrent List that were mentioned in the Instrument of Accession, namely Defence, Foreign Affairs, and Communications, and only after **consultation** with the Government of the State.
- Clause (ii) permitted Parliament to legislate on any other matters in the Union or Concurrent List, but only with the **concurrence** of the Government of Jammu and

Kashmir. This meant that laws on any subject outside the original scope of accession—such as education, civil procedure, or preventive detention—could not be applied unless the state government explicitly agreed.

The Significance of "Consultation" vs. "Concurrence"

The use of the terms "consultation" and "concurrence" in Article 370 was deliberate and constitutionally significant. These words had been interpreted differently in other parts of the Constitution and legal jurisprudence:

- Consultation implies that the Union government must seek the views of the State government, but is not necessarily bound by those views. It is a procedural requirement, not a substantive veto. Thus, on matters specified in the Instrument of Accession, the President could proceed after consulting the State—but need not obtain agreement.
- Concurrence, on the other hand, is much stronger. It implies explicit and affirmative agreement. Without the state's formal consent, the President could not extend a law or constitutional provision to Jammu and Kashmir on subjects outside the original Instrument of Accession.

The constitutional arrangement under Article 370(1)(b) clearly restricted the Indian Parliament's authority, ensuring that Jammu and Kashmir retained a distinctive legislative identity within the Union. However, legislative power was just one dimension of the state's special status. Equally critical was the question of which parts of the Indian Constitution would apply to Jammu and Kashmir, and how those provisions would be made applicable. This aspect is governed by the next two clauses of Article 370 — Clauses (c) and (d) — which together define the extent and manner of constitutional integration between the Union of India and the state.

Constitutional Application: Article 370(1)(c)

Article 370(1)(c) reads:

"The provisions of Article 1 and of this article shall apply in relation to that State."

This deceptively simple clause carries profound constitutional weight. It means that when the Constitution of India came into force on 26 January 1950, only two provisions of it automatically applied to Jammu and Kashmir:

- Article 1 – which defines India as a "Union of States" and includes Jammu and Kashmir as one of the constituent units listed in the First Schedule.
- Article 370 – which established the mechanism for defining and managing the constitutional relationship between the Union and the State of Jammu and Kashmir.

This was not a technical or procedural detail—it was a deliberate constitutional design. Unlike other princely states, whose integration into the Indian Union resulted in full constitutional incorporation, Jammu and Kashmir's inclusion was legally limited, cautious, and conditional. The accession was confined to three core subjects—defence, foreign affairs, and communications—and the constitutional reflection of that political agreement was enshrined in this clause.

Moreover, the express mention of only Article 1 and Article 370 in Clause (c) was also meant to emphasize that the entire remainder of the Constitution—Parts II to XXII—did not extend to Jammu and Kashmir by default. This included:

- Part III – Fundamental Rights
- Part IV – Directive Principles of State Policy
- Part V – The Union Executive
- Part VI – State Governments

And even provisions on citizenship, emergency powers, and inter-state commerce. In legal terms, this made Jammu and Kashmir's position constitutionally sui generis—a unique arrangement unlike any other Indian state, grounded in asymmetric federalism.

Hence the only constitutional relationship binding J&K to the Indian Union on 26 January 1950 was through:

- Its inclusion in the territory of India (Article 1), and
- The special federal framework established by Article 370 itself.

All other constitutional provisions required deliberate and consensual extension, which brings us to Clause (d).

Article 370(1)(d)

Article 370(1)(d) provides:

"Such of the other provisions of this Constitution shall apply in relation to that State subject to such exceptions and modifications as the President may by order specify:"

Provided that no such order which relates to matters specified in the Instrument of Accession shall be issued except in consultation with the Government of the State.

This clause was the operative gateway through which any further part of the Indian Constitution could be extended to Jammu and Kashmir. It empowered the President of India—not Parliament—to:

- Apply Indian constitutional provisions to J&K,
- Modify or exempt those provisions in their application,
- And crucially, do so only upon consultation or concurrence with the Government of the State, depending on the nature of the subject.

The distinction between "consultation" and "concurrence" here followed the same logic used in Article 370(1)(b):

- For matters within the Instrument of Accession (defence, foreign affairs, communications), consultation with the state government sufficed.
- For all other matters, the state's concurrence—i.e., formal and affirmative agreement—was required.

This gave the J&K government effective veto power over the application of any constitutional provision beyond those in the Accession.

Fundamental Rights Were Not Applicable by Default

Because Part III of the Indian Constitution—which enshrines Fundamental Rights—was not part of Article 1 or

370, it did not apply automatically to Jammu and Kashmir. For these rights to become enforceable in the state:

- The President had to invoke Article 370(1)(d) to issue a Presidential Order, and
- That order required the concurrence of the J&K Government, since Fundamental Rights were not included in the Instrument of Accession.

Consequence: Residents of Jammu and Kashmir did not originally enjoy the full scope of rights guaranteed to Indian citizens elsewhere, such as:

- Equality before law (Article 14)
- Freedom of speech (Article 19)
- Protection of life and liberty (Article 21)
- Safeguards against arbitrary arrest (Article 22)

It was only through the Constitution (Application to Jammu and Kashmir) Order, 1954, that the Union Government—with the State Government's concurrence—extended most of Part III to Jammu and Kashmir. However, this same order also introduced a new provision—Article 35A—which reinforced the state's autonomous power to define who qualified as a "permanent resident" and to confer upon them exclusive privileges, such as:

- The right to own land and property,
- Access to state government jobs,
- Eligibility for state welfare benefits and educational scholarships.

While Article 370(1) laid down the operational framework for determining which constitutional provisions could be extended to Jammu and Kashmir and under what procedural safeguards (consultation or concurrence), the drafters of the Constitution were also aware that this special arrangement was transitional in nature. It was expected that Jammu and Kashmir would frame its own Constitution, and that a Constituent Assembly would be set up in the state to determine the future course of its relationship with the Union of India. This brings us to the next important component — Article 370(2).

Role of Jammu and Kashmir constituent assembly

Text of Article 370(2):

"If the concurrence of the Government of the State referred to in paragraph (ii) of sub-clause (b) of clause (1) or in the second proviso to sub-clause (d) of that clause be given before the Constituent Assembly for the purpose of framing the Constitution of the State is convened, it shall be placed before such Assembly for such decision as it may take thereon."

This clause addresses a key transitional issue: what happens if the Government of Jammu and Kashmir gives its **concurrence** for the application of constitutional provisions or parliamentary laws before the State's Constituent Assembly is formed?

As per Article 370(1)(b)(ii) and 370(1)(d) second proviso, the President of India could extend constitutional provisions to Jammu and Kashmir with the concurrence of the State Government. However, in 1950, when the Indian Constitution came into effect, Jammu and Kashmir had not yet set up its own Constituent Assembly.The temporary Government (led by Sheikh Abdullah) was in place, but it was not elected by universal adult franchise, nor was it authorized to permanently decide constitutional matters.

So to ensure legitimacy and democratic validation, Article 370(2) mandated that: Any "concurrence" given by the interim government prior to the convening of the State's Constituent Assembly was provisional.

(please note : Article 370(2) of the Indian Constitution, the term "Government of the State" refers to the interim government of Jammu and Kashmir that existed before the State's Constituent Assembly was convened in 1951. After the signing of the Instrument of Accession in 1947, Jammu and Kashmir did not immediately have a democratically elected constituent body. Instead, the State was governed by an interim government, with Sheikh Abdullah functioning as Prime Minister under the authority of the Maharaja. During this interim period, certain provisions of the Indian Constitution were extended to J&K through Presidential Orders, based on the concurrence of this interim government. Article 370(2) recognized this transitional phase and mandated that any such concurrence given by the interim government before the Constituent Assembly was formed had to be placed before the Constituent Assembly once it was convened. This ensured democratic legitimacy and accountability once the elected body began functioning in October 1951.)

Such concurrence had to be placed before the State's Constituent Assembly once it was constituted. The Assembly could then review, ratify, modify, or reject those decisions. This clause institutionalized a check on early executive actions and ensured that the sovereign will of the people of Jammu and Kashmir, as represented through their Constituent Assembly, would have the final say on matters affecting the state's constitutional status. Hence it limited the power of the interim State Government, making its concurrence provisional and subject to future validation.

It reinforced the importance of democratic consent, consistent with the broader post-colonial emphasis on self-determination. It affirmed that permanent changes to Jammu and Kashmir's relationship with the Union must be made only with the approval of its Constituent Assembly.

While Article 370(2) ensured that the will of the Jammu and Kashmir Constituent Assembly would be the final arbiter on matters relating to the extension of constitutional provisions, the drafters also included a provision that addressed the potential termination or modification of the special status itself. However, this was not left to the discretion of Parliament or the executive alone. The power to abrogate or amend Article 370 in its entirety was made subject to a critical condition: the explicit recommendation of the State's Constituent Assembly. This brings us to the final and most consequential clause — Article 370(3).

Power to abrogate or modify article 370

Text of Article 370(3):

"Notwithstanding anything in the foregoing provisions of this article, the President may, by public notification, declare that this article shall cease to be operative or shall be operative only with such exceptions and modifications and from such date as he may specify:"

"Provided that the recommendation of the Constituent Assembly of the State referred to in clause (2) shall be necessary before the President issues such a notification."

This clause gives the President of India the formal power to:

- Declare Article 370 inoperative, i.e., abolish it entirely, or
- Modify its operation with specific exceptions or limitations.

However, there is one crucial caveat:
Such a Presidential declaration cannot be issued unilaterally. It requires the prior recommendation of the Constituent Assembly of Jammu and Kashmir — the very body discussed in Article 370(2).

Key Points of Article 370(3)

- Presidential Authority:
  The power to terminate or amend Article 370 lies not with Parliament but with the President, reinforcing the special, executive character of Article 370's application mechanism.
- Mandatory Precondition:
  The recommendation of the Jammu and Kashmir Constituent Assembly was a constitutional prerequisite. This means that:

1. No action under Article 370(3) could be taken without this recommendation.
2. Parliament or the Union Government could not bypass this requirement.

- Legal Finality: Since the J&K Constituent Assembly dissolved itself in 1957 without recommending abrogation, many legal scholars and judicial interpretations held that:

1. The condition in the proviso can no longer be fulfilled,
2. Therefore, Article 370 became permanent, despite being originally labeled a "temporary provision."

The constitutional architecture of Article 370 did not evolve in a vacuum. Over the decades, its interpretation, application, and eventual transformation were deeply influenced by a complex interplay of political decisions, institutional shifts, judicial pronouncements, and regional unrest. To fully understand the trajectory of Jammu and Kashmir's special status, it is essential to trace the critical political milestones and legal turning points that shaped its journey from conditional accession to complete constitutional integration — a journey marked by both gradual erosion and sudden rupture.

In October 1951, the Constituent Assembly of Jammu and Kashmir was formally convened with a threefold mandate: to frame the State's own Constitution, to determine the permanent constitutional status of Jammu and Kashmir within the Union of India, and to review and endorse the terms of accession along with any constitutional provisions extended under Article 370.

After more than five years of deliberation, the Assembly adopted the Constitution of Jammu and Kashmir on 26 November 1956, a date symbolically aligned with the adoption of the Indian Constitution in 1949. The Constitution officially came into force on 26 January 1957, deliberately chosen to coincide with India's Republic Day, reflecting a balance between state autonomy and national unity.

The Constitution of Jammu and Kashmir asserted that the state was an integral part of the Union of India, yet it maintained distinctive features: **a separate flag, its own definition of citizenship, and a bicameral legislature.** Importantly, unlike other Indian states where residuary powers lie with the Union, the J&K Constitution vested these powers in the State Legislature, further reinforcing its special status. Later in 1957, the Constituent Assembly dissolved itself, having completed its work. Notably, it did not make any recommendation regarding the abrogation or amendment of Article 370, as required under Article 370(3) of the Indian Constitution.

While the Constituent Assembly was shaping the constitutional identity of Jammu and Kashmir, equally significant were the parallel political developments that reshaped the region's leadership, governance structure, and relationship with the Indian Union. These events, particularly involving Sheikh Abdullah, the Dogra monarchy, and Prime Minister Nehru, would lay the foundation for both the symbolic assertion of Kashmir's autonomy and the seeds of later instability.

After Maharaja Hari Singh signed the Instrument of Accession in October 1947, his role in the political affairs of Jammu and Kashmir rapidly diminished. In a symbolic yet politically charged shift, he declared Sheikh Abdullah as the interim Prime Minister (Wazir-e-Azam) of Jammu and Kashmir. However, tensions between the two were immediate and irreconcilable. Hari Singh, who had once ruled as an autocratic monarch, now found himself marginalized in a system led by a popular mass leader.

According to political accounts, Abdullah bluntly told Hari Singh to step aside and leave the political scene. The public too reacted with discomfort to this abrupt transition, recognizing the moment as a decisive break from princely rule to popular government.

To manage the political fallout, Hari Singh relinquished his position and nominated his son, Karan Singh, as the Prince Regent in 1949, effectively transferring ceremonial duties and aligning with the emerging constitutional order. This symbolic move marked the end of monarchic power and the formal beginning of representative governance in the state.

In 1952, as Sheikh Abdullah consolidated his political base and popular legitimacy, he entered into direct negotiations with Prime Minister Nehru, resulting in what is known as the Delhi Agreement. Abdullah made several demands during these talks, seeking clarity and reaffirmation of Jammu and Kashmir's autonomous status. These included:

- Recognition of the state's head of state as Sadr-i-Riyasat, to be elected by the State Legislature instead of being appointed by the President of India;
- Retaining the title of Prime Minister (Wazir-e-Azam) for the state's executive head;
- Safeguards on Kashmir's demographic composition, including protections around land ownership and settlement rights;
- Continued enforcement of laws that restricted land ownership and citizenship to permanent residents.

Nehru agreed to these demands, seeking to preserve India's secular and democratic image and to strengthen the

Union's bond with Kashmir through accommodation rather than coercion.

Despite the Delhi Agreement, political trust began to erode. Abdullah's growing charisma, mass appeal, and ambiguous statements about the possibility of Kashmir's independent future began to raise concerns within the Indian establishment. His references to self-determination, although vague, were interpreted by many in Delhi as signs of separatist inclinations.

On 8 August 1953, in a dramatic political development, Sadr-i-Riyasat Karan Singh, who had by then replaced the Prince Regent title, backed the dismissal of Sheikh Abdullah in what was effectively a coup d'état. Abdullah was removed from office and arrested under the pretext of harboring aspirations for an independent Kashmir. This event, known as the Kashmir Conspiracy Case, led to his imprisonment for nearly eleven years, sparking both regional unrest and national controversy.

Although this move was legally justified by the authority of the Sadr-i-Riyasat, many scholars and political commentators view it as a Delhi-backed intervention aimed at neutralizing a leader who, despite being central to Kashmir's accession, had grown politically unpredictable. The aftermath of this decision deeply damaged the political legitimacy of the Indian state in Kashmir and laid the groundwork for the growing alienation of sections of the Kashmiri population in the decades to follow.

In the aftermath of Sheikh Abdullah's arrest in 1953, political power in Jammu and Kashmir shifted decisively toward the Centre's influence. This realignment created the conditions for a critical legal development in the state's constitutional history. While the Constituent Assembly of Jammu and Kashmir was still in session and under an administration more amenable to New Delhi, the Union Government moved to expand the constitutional framework applicable to the state. The result was the Presidential Order of 1954, a sweeping executive action that not only extended large parts of the Indian Constitution to Jammu and Kashmir but also inserted a unique and controversial provision—Article 35A—into the legal fabric of the Constitution itself.

On 14 May 1954, the President of India issued the Constitution (Application to Jammu and Kashmir) Order, 1954 under Article 370(1)(d), with the concurrence of the State Government (then headed by Bakshi Ghulam Mohammad after Abdullah's arrest). This Presidential Order was the most comprehensive of its kind and marked a watershed moment in J&K's constitutional history. Among other things, it extended:

- Most of Part III (Fundamental Rights) of the Constitution,
- Provisions relating to the Supreme Court, Election Commission, and Comptroller and Auditor General, and
- Select entries from the Union and Concurrent Lists.

But the most significant and contentious feature of the 1954 Order was the insertion of a new provision—Article 35A—into the Appendix of the Constitution of India.Article 35A empowered the Jammu and Kashmir Legislature to:

- Define who is a "permanent resident" of the state,
- Confer upon such permanent residents special rights and privileges in:

1. Employment under the State Government,
2. Acquisition of immovable property in the state,
3. Access to scholarships and public welfare,
4. Other forms of public aid and benefits.

This meant that non-permanent residents (including Indian citizens from other states) could not purchase property, secure government jobs, or access certain state-funded benefits in Jammu and Kashmir.

- Article 35A was not added through a constitutional amendment under Article 368, which would have required passage by a two-thirds majority in both Houses of Parliament.
- Instead, it was inserted via the Presidential Order of 1954, using Article 370(1)(d)—a mechanism that allowed the President to extend and modify constitutional provisions for Jammu and Kashmir with the concurrence of the State Government, but without Parliament's formal involvement.
- It was placed in the Appendix to the Constitution, not in the main body, and hence:

1. Article 35A does not appear in the original numbered Articles of the Constitution.
2. It can be overlooked in casual readings, as it was appended as a presidential insertion outside the standard legislative process.

Article 35A became an executive constitutional provision, made possible exclusively through the special powers granted by Article 370, reinforcing both J&K's autonomy and the extraordinary flexibility Article 370 provided for legal integration.

Following the 1954 Presidential Order and the adoption of the Jammu and Kashmir Constitution in 1956, the state enjoyed a considerable degree of constitutional autonomy. However, over the next two decades, this autonomy was gradually eroded through a series of Presidential Orders and executive actions, often enacted during periods of political instability. A key milestone in this process came in 1964, when the President of India extended Article 356—pertaining to President's Rule—to Jammu and Kashmir, thereby creating a constitutional pathway for direct Central intervention in the state's governance.

In 1964, the Constitution (Application to Jammu and Kashmir) Order, 1954 was amended by a Presidential Order to extend Article 356 of the Indian Constitution to the state. This article empowers the President of India to impose President's Rule in a state when the constitutional machinery breaks down. Its extension to J&K was a major shift, as it allowed the Union Government to directly administer the state in times of political crisis, even though J&K had its own mechanisms under its Constitution.

Though technically made possible under Article 370(1)(d), the 1964 extension of Article 356 marked a further assimilation of Jammu and Kashmir into the broader Indian constitutional structure, reducing the distinctiveness originally preserved in the post-accession arrangement.

To fully appreciate the implications of such changes, it is important to understand the Constitution of Jammu and Kashmir, which came into effect on 26 January 1957. This document was a product of the state's Constituent Assembly and was intended to reflect the unique historical, political, and cultural identity of the region within the

Indian Union.

Key Features of the Jammu and Kashmir Constitution

The Constitution of Jammu and Kashmir, which came into effect on 26 January 1957, was a comprehensive legal document with:

- 158 Articles,
- Divided into 13 Parts, and
- Supplemented by 7 Schedules.

Among its most significant features were the following provisions:

- Article 3 of the J&K Constitution:
Declares unequivocally that *"The State of Jammu and Kashmir is and shall be an integral part of the Union of India."*
This declaration mirrored the Indian Constitution's position and reasserted the finality of accession.
- Article 4:
Definedo the territorial extent of the state, including all territories under the sovereignty or suzerainty of the Maharaja as of 15 August 1947, thereby maintaining a symbolic claim over Pakistan-administered Kashmir.
- Article 5:
Delineated the division of powers, stating that the executive and legislative authority of the state extended to all matters except those explicitly assigned to Parliament under the Constitution of India. This was a restatement of the autonomy model under Article 370,

affirming that Parliament could only legislate on J&K matters in limited circumstances.

Articles 6–10: Permanent Resident Rights and Article 35A

Articles 6 to 10 of the J&K Constitution dealt with the definition, rights, and obligations of "permanent residents" of the state. These articles:

- Gave the J&K Legislature exclusive authority to define and regulate the rights of permanent residents,
- Provided special privileges in land ownership, government employment, education, and welfare,
- Created a statutory and constitutional framework to implement Article 35A, which had been inserted into the Indian Constitution through the 1954 Presidential Order.

Together, these provisions codified the special status of J&K residents and formed a legal barrier against the full application of Indian laws on property and citizenship within the state.

Section 92: Emergency Powers Under the J&K Constitution

In addition to the now-applicable Article 356 of the Indian Constitution, Section 92 of the J&K Constitution provided an internal mechanism for handling political instability within the state itself. Under this section:

- The Governor could declare a constitutional breakdown in the functioning of the state government.
- Upon such a declaration, the Governor was empowered to:

1. Assume executive functions of the state,
2. Suspend provisions of the state constitution (excluding those related to High Court powers),
3. Govern the state with the concurrence of the President of India.

- Such a proclamation had to be placed before the state legislature, and could remain in force for six months, with the possibility of extension or revocation.

This provision was unique to J&K and served as a parallel emergency provision to Article 356. However, once Article 356 was applied in 1964, Section 92 began to lose relevance in practice, as the Union Government increasingly used Article 356 to impose President's Rule—particularly during politically sensitive or unstable periods.

By the mid-1960s, the cumulative impact of Presidential Orders and political developments had significantly altered the federal balance between Jammu and Kashmir and the Union of India. The initial framework under Article 370 had allowed for limited integration—only with the State Government's concurrence—but successive modifications steadily expanded the Union's constitutional footprint. One of the most symbolic and politically consequential of these changes came in 1965, when the nomenclature of the state's highest executive and constitutional offices—a powerful expression of Kashmir's distinctiveness—was brought into line with those of other Indian states.

Abolition of Sadr-i-Riyasat and Wazir-e-Azam

In 1965, the Constitution (Application to Jammu and Kashmir) Second Amendment Order, 1965 was issued under Article 370(1)(d) by the President of India, with the concurrence of the J&K Government. This Presidential Order made a substantive change to the Jammu and Kashmir Constitution by replacing:

- The title of "Sadr-i-Riyasat" (Head of State) with "Governor", and
- The title of "Wazir-e-Azam" (Prime Minister) with "Chief Minister".

These terms—used nowhere else in India—were central to Kashmir's political identity post-accession. Their replacement marked:

- The symbolic loss of political distinctiveness,
- The administrative assimilation of J&K into the constitutional mold of other Indian states,
- And a consolidation of the Union's control, particularly because the new Governor would now be appointed by the President of India, not elected by the J&K legislature as the Sadr-i-Riyasat had been.

This change also reflected the Central Government's growing influence over Kashmir's internal governance, especially after the political fallout from Sheikh Abdullah's dismissal in 1953.

By the early 1970s, the political dynamics around Jammu and Kashmir had shifted significantly—both regionally and globally. The Bangladesh Liberation War of 1971, which ended with India's decisive victory and the creation of Bangladesh, reshaped the subcontinental power balance. Within this new geopolitical context, Sheikh Abdullah, who had spent over a decade politically marginalized, began to reassess his position. What followed was a series of backchannel negotiations, public signals, and eventually a historic political reconciliation between Sheikh Abdullah and Prime Minister Indira Gandhi, culminating in the 1975 Indira–Abdullah Accord.

India's military victory over Pakistan in December 1971, and the subsequent creation of Bangladesh, drastically altered South Asia's strategic environment.Pakistan's defeat significantly weakened its claim over Kashmir in the international arena.Sheikh Abdullah, who had long championed the idea of a plebiscite under UN resolutions, found himself in a reduced bargaining position, as the global momentum shifted against Pakistan's Kashmir claims.

In early 1972, Sheikh Abdullah gave a notable interview to The Times (London), where he reiterated his long-held stance on a plebiscite, but his tone had notably softened.Observers, including the Indian government, interpreted this shift as a sign that Abdullah was becoming more pragmatic and flexible, given the altered political reality post-1971.

Indira Gandhi, recognizing this shift, kept channels of communication open, seeing potential for reintegration of Abdullah into the constitutional framework.In the years that followed, informal negotiations were initiated between: Mirza Afzal Beg, a close confidant of Sheikh Abdullah and founder of the Plebiscite Front, and Gopalaswami Parthasarathi, a seasoned diplomat and close aide of Indira Gandhi.These meetings were low-profile, held outside the media spotlight, and aimed at bridging the gap between Abdullah's constitutional reservations and the Indian government's insistence on Kashmir's final integration. The key points of discussion included:

- Whether Abdullah would accept the accession as final,
- The status of Article 370, and
- The extent of legislative and administrative autonomy that could be restored or preserved.

February 1975: The Indira–Abdullah Accord

After nearly years of negotiation, a formal understanding was reached and announced in February 1975. Commonly referred to as the Indira–Abdullah Accord, it was not a signed treaty, but rather a mutually agreed memorandum between the parties, tabled in both the Indian Parliament and the J&K Legislative Assembly.

Key Provisions of the Accord:

- Finality of Accession:

1. Sheikh Abdullah accepted that Jammu and Kashmir is an integral part of the Union of India.
2. The Instrument of Accession was deemed final and irrevocable.
3. The plebiscite demand was officially abandoned.

- Retention of Article 370:

1. Article 370 would continue to serve as the constitutional bridge between Jammu and Kashmir and the Union of India.

2. It remained the mechanism through which any future constitutional provisions could be applied to the state.

- Status of Existing Central Laws:

1. All constitutional provisions and central laws that had been extended to J&K before 1975 would remain in force.
2. The J&K Legislature could review and recommend modifications to some of these laws, but any such change would be subject to the President of India's approval—as per Article 370(1)(d).

- Future Legislative Autonomy:

1. No rollback of existing integration was promised.
2. Future discussions on state autonomy would remain within the framework of the Indian Constitution, and the Parliament's authority would not be diluted.

- Restoration of Political Power:

1. In return, Prime Minister Indira Gandhi agreed to reintegrate Sheikh Abdullah into constitutional politics.
2. The then Chief Minister, Syed Mir Qasim, resigned to facilitate this process.
3. On 25 February 1975, Sheikh Abdullah was sworn in as the Chief Minister of Jammu and Kashmir, marking his return to power after 22 years.

Although the 1975 Indira–Abdullah Accord marked a major political reconciliation between Sheikh Abdullah and the Indian government, the underlying tensions in Jammu and Kashmir's political landscape remained unresolved. While Sheikh Abdullah's return to power temporarily stabilized the situation, his passing in 1982 marked the end of an era. His son, Farooq Abdullah, inherited both the leadership of the National Conference and the burden of navigating a complex relationship with New Delhi.

What followed was a period of increasing political intrigue, shifting alliances, and growing interference from the Centre—culminating in the controversial dismissal of Farooq Abdullah in 1984, which would sow deeper mistrust and pave the way for future unrest . Farooq Abdullah was dismissed as Chief Minister despite having a majority. His brother-in-law Ghulam Mohammad Shah was installed with the support of defectors, triggering widespread public anger and a legitimacy crisis. This event is widely considered one of the key turning points that eroded public trust in electoral democracy in J&K, contributing to political alienation. In the 1987 J&K Assembly elections, Farooq Abdullah's National Conference (NC) entered an alliance with the Indian National Congress (INC).

The election was allegedly rigged in several constituencies to defeat the Muslim United Front (MUF), an emerging coalition of Islamist and political groups.The widespread perception of fraud led to deep disillusionment, especially among Kashmiri youth. Key MUF figures—including Yusuf Shah (later Syed Salahuddin) and Mohammad Yasin Malik—joined or led militant outfits, and by 1989, an armed insurgency had erupted. In January 1990, in response to the escalating violence, the Governor of J&K, Jagmohan, imposed Governor's Rule under Section 92 of the J&K Constitution. Mass protests, killings, and the exodus of the Kashmiri Pandit community followed.

Democratic processes remained suspended; President's Rule under Article 356 was imposed later that year. In July 1990, the Armed Forces (Jammu and Kashmir) Special Powers Act (AFSPA) was enacted via Parliamentary legislation, empowering the armed forces to: Use force, arrest without warrant, and conduct operations in "disturbed areas", Grant legal immunity to personnel for actions taken in good faith. AFSPA was applied first to the Kashmir Valley, and later extended to Jammu region. While justified by the Centre as necessary to combat militancy, it has been deeply controversial, accused of fostering human rights violations and impunity. After six years of President's Rule, Assembly elections were held in 1996. Farooq Abdullah returned as Chief Minister.The elections marked a partial return to normalcy, but political alienation and militancy continued in various forms.

Under the NDA-I government led by Atal Bihari Vajpayee, efforts were made to normalize relations with Pakistan and engage with separatists.Vajpayee's "Insaaniyat, Jamhooriyat, Kashmiriyat" doctrine emphasized: Respecting human rights (Insaaniyat),Strengthening democracy (Jamhooriyat), Preserving the cultural ethos of Kashmir (Kashmiriyat). Dialogue was initiated with separatist groups, and cross-border bus services (e.g., Srinagar–Muzaffarabad) were launched.This period saw a dip in violence and public engagement with electoral processes began to improve.

Amarnath Land Row and Political Volatility

- The decision to transfer land to the Amarnath Shrine Board triggered massive protests in the Kashmir Valley, followed by counter-protests in Jammu.

- The unrest led to the fall of the PDP–Congress coalition, headed by Ghulam Nabi Azad.
- The region experienced deep communal and regional polarization, setting the stage for new alignments.
- The National Conference (Farooq and Omar Abdullah) allied with the Congress in 2009.
- Omar Abdullah became Chief Minister, but his tenure was marred by: the 2010 summer unrest (over 100 deaths in protests), A perception of inaccessibility and administrative rigidity.
- The Centre under UPA II initiated some confidence-building measures, but no substantive political breakthrough occurred.

BJP Enters Power in Delhi and Kashmir

- In 2014, the BJP won a national majority under Narendra Modi, and also performed strongly in the J&K Assembly elections, especially in Jammu.
- Despite ideological differences, a coalition was formed with the People's Democratic Party (PDP), led by Mufti Mohammad Sayeed.
- This BJP–PDP alliance was dubbed an "Alliance of Opposites", combining BJP's integrationist stance with PDP's regional autonomy agenda.
- After Mufti Mohammad Sayeed's death in January 2016, his daughter Mehbooba Mufti took over as Chief Minister.
- The coalition came under increasing strain due to : the 2016 killing of Burhan Wani (a Hizbul Mujahideen

commander), which led to months of violent protests and civilian deaths. Differences in political vision—BJP pushed for tighter integration, while PDP tried to preserve regional autonomy. Governance became increasingly ineffective amid growing alienation in the Valley.

- On 19 June 2018, the BJP unilaterally pulled out of the coalition, citing security failures and ideological incompatibility.

The collapse of the BJP–PDP coalition in June 2018 marked a decisive turning point in Jammu and Kashmir's political trajectory. With no party or alliance able to form a government, the state was once again placed under direct central control. This time, however, the situation unfolded against the backdrop of growing political centralization and speculation about significant constitutional changes. The use of Governor's Rule under the J&K Constitution, followed by a swift shift to President's Rule, signaled not only administrative breakdown but also a prelude to far-reaching decisions that would soon transform the constitutional identity of Jammu and Kashmir. As the BJP withdrew support from the ruling PDP–BJP coalition, effectively ending Mehbooba Mufti's government, the very next day, on 20 June 2018, Governor's Rule was imposed under Section 92 of the Jammu and Kashmir Constitution, which was still in force at the time. Section 92 of the J&K Constitution authorized the Governor to assume all powers of the state when he was satisfied that the government could not function in accordance with the Constitution. The Governor could:take over executive functions, Suspend or dissolve the Legislative Assembly, and Legislate by ordinance. However, any proclamation under Section

92 required the concurrence of the President of India, and had to be laid before the State Legislature (if in session). Importantly, the provision itself did not provide for any extension beyond six months.

Why This Was Significant

- Unlike Article 356 of the Indian Constitution, which allows for the extension of President's Rule, Section 92 had no legal mechanism for continuation beyond six months.
- Therefore, if normalcy wasn't restored within that period, the only legal recourse was to invoke Article 356 and impose President's Rule. Just two days before Governor's Rule was set to expire, the Union Cabinet recommended the imposition of President's Rule under Article 356 of the Constitution of India.
- On 19 December 2018, the President of India issued a proclamation imposing President's Rule in Jammu and Kashmir, bringing the state fully under central control.
- Under President's Rule, the Governor became the agent of the President, and all legislative powers of the Assembly were vested in Parliament.
- This move marked the end of the J&K Constitution's operational role in managing breakdowns of governance, as Section 92 became moot with the imposition of Article 356.

By late 2018, with the imposition of President's Rule under Article 356 and the dissolution of the J&K Legislative Assembly, Jammu and Kashmir was entirely under direct central control. With no elected government in place, the constitutional requirement for "concurrence" or "consultation" with the state government—as prescribed under Article 370—became a point of interpretation rather than an institutional check. Against this backdrop, on 5 August 2019, the Government of India launched a multi-stage constitutional operation that would result in the effective abrogation of Article 370, ending Jammu and Kashmir's special status. This began with the issuance of a Presidential Order—C.O. 272—through a reinterpretation of the Constitution itself.

The Constitution (Application to Jammu and Kashmir) Order, 2019—C.O. 272

On 5 August 2019, the Ministry of Law and Justice (Legislative Department) issued a notification publishing the Constitution (Application to Jammu and Kashmir) Order, 2019—C.O. 272, made under Article 370(1) of the Constitution of India.

This order declared that:

"In exercise of the powers conferred by clause (1) of article 370 of the Constitution, the President, with the concurrence of the Government of State of Jammu and Kashmir, is pleased to make the following Order..."

The 1954 Presidential Order, which had governed the constitutional relationship between India and J&K for over 65 years—including the insertion of Article 35A—was explicitly superseded. All provisions of the Indian Constitution were now to apply in full to Jammu and Kashmir, without exceptions or modifications, unless specifically stated.

The most critical—and controversial—aspect of C.O. 272 was the amendment to Article 367, which deals with the interpretation of the Constitution. Article 367 incorporates, by reference, provisions of the General Clauses Act, which helps interpret statutory language across Indian laws.

A new sub-clause (4) was inserted to redefine key expressions used in Article 370, as they apply to Jammu and Kashmir:

- Interpretation Clause:

All references to "the Constitution" were clarified to mean "as applied to the State of Jammu and Kashmir." Now, by inserting this interpretation into Article 367, the government created legal clarity (and justification) for: treating the Constitution as fully applicable to J&K, superseding the earlier limited or conditional application;

1. Enabling reinterpretation of terms used in Article 370 itself (like "Constituent Assembly" or "State Government") based on the Constitution as now fully applied to J&K;
2. Shifting constitutional interpretation away from historical exceptions and treating J&K like any other Indian state—despite Article 370 still technically being in place at that moment.

- Sadr-i-Riyasat = Governor:

The term *"Sadr-i-Riyasat"* (used in Article 370(3)) was reinterpreted as "Governor of Jammu and Kashmir", who was at that time acting under President's Rule.

- Government of the State = Governor:

1. The term *"Government of the State"*, used in Article 370(1), was now to be read as the Governor of Jammu and Kashmir acting on the advice of his Council of Ministers—which did not exist since the Assembly had been dissolved.
2. Thus, the Governor alone was treated as "the Government", enabling him to give "concurrence" on behalf of the state.

Lets clear confusion which might arise here. Article 370(1) (d) of the Indian Constitution says that constitutional provisions can be applied to Jammu and Kashmir with "consultation" or "concurrence" of the Government of the State, depending on the subject. Normally, the "Government of the State" refers to:

1. An elected government of Jammu and Kashmir,
2. Headed by a Chief Minister and a Council of Ministers, who advise the Governor (like in any other state of India).

This requirement ensured that no constitutional change could be made without involving the elected government of Jammu and Kashmir—a key part of the autonomy granted under Article 370. On 5 August 2019, the President issued Constitution Order C.O. 272. This added a new clause to Article 367, which is used to interpret constitutional language. This clause redefined "Government of the State" to mean:

"The Governor of Jammu and Kashmir acting on the advice of his Council of Ministers." But at that time:

1. The state government had been dissolved,

2. There was no Chief Minister or Council of Ministers,
3. Jammu and Kashmir was under President's Rule, with the Governor acting as the sole authority under instructions from the Centre.

So in practice, this meant: the Governor alone was now legally treated as the "Government of the State" even though he had no elected government to advise him. This reinterpretation allowed the Governor (a centrally appointed official) to give the required "concurrence" on behalf of the state,even though there was no elected state government to consult, Which made it possible for the President to issue C.O. 272, applying all provisions of the Indian Constitution to J&K. Without this change, the Centre would have needed the formal consent of an elected J&K government, which did not exist at the time.

Now, a question may arise—if Constitution Order (C.O.) 272 was issued under Article 370(1)(d), and at that time the Governor was functioning as the State Government due to President's Rule under Article 356, then why was it necessary to reinterpret the term "Government of the State" within the same Order to mean the Governor? Wasn't the Governor already exercising that authority under Article 356?

Under Article 370(1)(d), the President of India could apply provisions of the Indian Constitution to Jammu & Kashmir only with the concurrence of the "Government of the State." In August 2019, Jammu & Kashmir was under President's Rule, and hence, the Governor—acting on behalf of the President—provided the required concurrence for issuing Constitution Order (C.O.) 272. At first glance, it may appear redundant or unnecessary to reinterpret the term "Government of the State" within C.O.

272, since the Governor had already exercised that authority.However, the reinterpretation was legally necessary for the following reasons:

Convention vs. Codification:

1. The Governor's role as the "Government of the State" during President's Rule was based on constitutional convention and judicial recognition, not on explicit constitutional language.
2. Such conventions are subject to legal scrutiny unless formally codified.
3. Redefining "Government of the State" within C.O. 272 (via Article 367) gave explicit legal backing to the Governor's authority in this context.

To Avoid Future Legal Challenges:

1. The process of abrogating Article 370 was a major constitutional change.
2. Any ambiguity in the interpretation of terms like "Government of the State" could lead to judicial challenges.
3. The reinterpretation helped ensure that the action was seen as constitutionally valid, not just politically executable.

Foundation for Reinterpreting Other Terms:

1. C.O. 272 also redefined other crucial terms like "Sadr-i-Riyasat" and "Constituent Assembly".
2. These reinterpretations were essential to proceed with the next step—invoking Article 370(3)—which required the recommendation of the Constituent Assembly

(which no longer existed).

3. A consistent reinterpretation framework required redefining all relevant terms, including "Government of the State".

Although the Governor gave concurrence to issue C.O. 272, the term "Government of the State" had never been explicitly equated with the Governor in the Constitution. Hence, C.O. 272 redefined it using Article 367 to formally legalize the Governor's role in the abrogation process and to make the entire procedure constitutionally robust and judicially defensible.

Now, another question may arise—if the Governor's concurrence under Article 370(1)(d) was a prerequisite for issuing Constitution Order (C.O.) 272, how was that concurrence validly obtained when the reinterpretation of the term "Government of the State"—to mean the Governor—was introduced within the same order itself? Wouldn't that create a logical inconsistency in the sequence of events, especially considering that the Governor was functioning as the State Government only due to President's Rule under Article 356?

So the issuance of Constitution Order (C.O.) 272 on 5th August 2019 amended Article 367 as applicable to Jammu & Kashmir, redefining "Government of the State" under Article 370(1)(d) to mean the Governor acting on the aid and advice of the President. This reinterpretation was crucial because the Governor's concurrence to the application of constitutional provisions, including Article 370(3), had been given before C.O. 272 was issued.

1. Article 367 – Interpretation Clause: C.O. 272 amended Article 367, incorporating a legal fiction that

"Government of the State" shall include the Governor. Although the concurrence occurred before this change, the reinterpretation became effective immediately upon issuance, creating a self-validating legal framework.

2. Doctrine of Contemporaneous Interpretation: This doctrine allows terms to be defined at the moment of execution. The concurrent reinterpretation of "Government of the State" and the act requiring such interpretation were contemporaneous, rendering the Governor's prior concurrence functionally valid.

3. Doctrine of Necessity: The Governor, acting on behalf of the President, was the only authority available to fulfill constitutional requirements. This necessity justified the action and was later formalized through C.O. 272.

4. Doctrine of Legal Fictions: C.O. 272 constructed a legal fiction redefining the term "Government" for constitutional purposes. Legal fictions, when explicitly created, are binding and enable retroactive validation of acts that rely upon them.

While the Governor's concurrence under Article 370(1)(d) technically preceded the reinterpretation of "Government of the State," Constitution Order (C.O.) 272 simultaneously redefined the term within the same legal instrument. This self-referential mechanism created a constitutionally defensible structure, resolving the apparent temporal anomaly through established constitutional doctrines and interpretive legitimacy.

The Supreme Court, in In Re: Article 370 (2023), upheld the validity of this process. During President's Rule in Jammu & Kashmir, imposed in December 2018 under Article 356, the Governor was constitutionally empowered to act in place of the elected state government. The Court held that C.O. 272's amendment to Article 367—which interpreted "Government of the State" as referring to the Governor—contemporaneously validated the concurrence through a legal fiction. The concurrence and reinterpretation, occurring within the same constitutional order, were treated as a single, integrated act.

This action was upheld using the Doctrine of Necessity to justify the Governor's role, the Doctrine of Legal Fiction to support the definitional shift, and the Doctrine of Contemporaneous Interpretation to align the meaning of the term at the time of the order's issuance. Though the move was not without constitutional controversy, the Court found no procedural irregularity and affirmed the President's power under Article 370(1)(d) to issue C.O. 272.

- Legislative Assembly = Constituent Assembly:

The proviso to Article 370(3) originally required that the recommendation of the Jammu and Kashmir Constituent Assembly was necessary before the President could declare Article 370 inoperative. However, through the Constitution (Application to Jammu and Kashmir) Order, 2019 (C.O. 272) issued on 5 August 2019, a new clause (4) was inserted into Article 367—which governs the interpretation of constitutional terms. This clause redefined key expressions used in Article 370, including interpreting "Constituent Assembly of the State referred to in clause (2)" to mean the "Legislative Assembly of the State". However, since no Legislative Assembly was in existence at that time due to President's Rule, the powers of the State Legislature are exercised by the Parliament of India. This principle is well-established in Indian constitutional practice.

Under President's Rule, the President assumes the functions of the state government, and Parliament assumes the powers of the state legislature, typically exercised through both Houses. By reinterpreting "Constituent Assembly" as "Legislative Assembly" under Article 367, and Considering that there was no Legislative Assembly in place, and under President's Rule, the Parliament effectively functioned as the Legislative Assembly,this created a complete legal pathway for the Union Government to: fulfill the procedural requirement of Article 370(3), without needing recommendation or ratification from any elected body in J&K.Thus, the reinterpreted Article 370(3) proviso—which had originally required the recommendation of the now-dissolved J&K Constituent Assembly—was now read as requiring a recommendation from the Legislative Assembly, which in turn was substituted by Parliament under Article 356.

This formed the legal basis for what followed on 6 August 2019: the Presidential Order (C.O. 273) formally declaring Article 370 inoperative, and the introduction and passage of the Jammu and Kashmir Reorganisation Act, 2019, which bifurcated the state into two Union Territories—Jammu & Kashmir (with a legislature) and Ladakh (without a legislature).

On 6 August 2019, the Union Government took the final legal step to render Article 370 inoperative by introducing a formal resolution under Article 370(3) in the Rajya Sabha.

The constitutional text of Article 370(3) reads:

"Notwithstanding anything in the foregoing provisions of this article, the President may, by public notification, declare that this article shall cease to be operative or shall

be operative only with such exceptions and modifications and from such date as he may specify:
Provided that the recommendation of the Constituent Assembly of the State referred to in clause (2) shall be necessary before the President issues such a notification."

This proviso had, for decades, been considered the legal barrier preventing unilateral abrogation of Article 370, as the Constituent Assembly of Jammu and Kashmir dissolved in 1957 without recommending repeal.

However, as explained earlier, the Constitution (Application to Jammu and Kashmir) Order, 2019 (C.O. 272), issued on 5 August 2019, had redefined key terms in Article 370 by inserting clause (4) to Article 367, which deals with constitutional interpretation.Specifically:

- "Constituent Assembly" was reinterpreted as "Legislative Assembly" (per Article 367(4)(d)),
- Since no Legislative Assembly was in existence due to President's Rule under Article 356,
- The Parliament of India—which exercises the powers of the state legislature during President's Rule—was treated as the Legislative Assembly for this purpose.

Therefore, the requirement in the proviso to Article 370(3)—that the President must have the recommendation of the "Constituent Assembly"—was legally satisfied through this layered mechanism:

- Constituent Assembly → Legislative Assembly (via Article 367),
- Legislative Assembly → Parliament (via Article 356).

Based on this legal interpretation, Union Home Minister Amit Shah introduced the following resolution in the Rajya Sabha on 6 August 2019:

"That this House recommends the following public notification to be issued by the President of India under Article 370(3): *In exercise of the powers conferred by clause (3) of Article 370 of the Constitution, the President, on the recommendation of the Parliament, hereby declares that all clauses of the said Article 370 shall cease to be operative, except clause (1) thereof.*"

This resolution was passed by both Houses of Parliament (Rajya Sabha on 5 August and Lok Sabha on 6 August 2019), fulfilling the final procedural requirement for the President to act under Article 370(3).

Following the resolution, the President issued Constitution Order C.O. 273, officially declaring that Article 370 (except clause (1) was inoperative. Clause (1) remained only for historical purposes to validate the application of the Indian Constitution to Jammu and Kashmir going forward. To avoid any technical confusion, it is important to understand that Article 370 of the Indian Constitution was legally and officially rendered inoperative on 6 August 2019.

The process, however, began a day earlier. On 5 August 2019, the President of India issued Constitution Order C.O. 272 under Article 370(1), which did not abrogate Article 370 but fundamentally altered its interpretation. This was achieved by inserting a new sub-clause in Article 367—the interpretative clause of the Constitution. Through this, the terms "Constituent Assembly" in Article 370(3) were redefined to mean "Legislative Assembly," and, since Jammu and Kashmir was under President's Rule (Article 356), the Legislative Assembly was constitutionally substituted by Parliament. Similarly, "Government of the State" was reinterpreted to mean the Governor, acting on behalf of the Centre. These changes laid the legal groundwork for action under Article 370(3).

The next day, on 6 August 2019, Parliament passed a resolution under Article 370(3) recommending the abrogation of Article 370, and based on this, the President issued Constitution Order C.O. 273, which declared that all clauses of Article 370 shall cease to be operative, except clause (1). This formal Presidential notification marked the legal point at which Article 370 became inoperative. Thus, while 5 August initiated the process through reinterpretation and application of constitutional tools, it was 6 August 2019 that marked the actual and technical abrogation of the special status of Jammu and Kashmir.

With the successful passage of the first resolution rendering Article 370 inoperative (except for clause (1)), Jammu and Kashmir's constitutional status was fundamentally altered. This shift had immediate legal consequences: it removed the special procedural safeguards that had previously restricted the Union Government's ability to make structural changes to the state. Most importantly, it enabled the application of Article 3 of the Indian Constitution to Jammu and Kashmir—something that had not been possible under the old Article 370 framework without state concurrence. This cleared the path for the introduction of a second resolution and a landmark legislative bill: the Jammu and Kashmir Reorganisation Bill, 2019, which sought to bifurcate the state and downgrade its status.

Following the passage of the first resolution under Article 370(3), Union Home Minister Amit Shah moved a second resolution on 6 August 2019, recommending the reorganisation of the State of Jammu and Kashmir into two Union Territories. This resolution was accompanied by the introduction of the Jammu and Kashmir Reorganisation Bill, 2019.

Article 3 of the Indian Constitution empowers Parliament to:

"Form a new State by separation of territory from any State or by uniting two or more States or parts of States... increase the area of any State... diminish the area of any State... alter the boundaries or names of any State."

However, prior to 5 August 2019, Article 3 was not freely applicable to Jammu and Kashmir because of:

- Article 370(1)(d): Constitutional provisions, including Article 3, had to be separately applied to J&K via Presidential Orders;
- And Section 147 of the J&K Constitution, which prohibited any alteration of the state's boundaries or status.

Once Article 370 was rendered inoperative, Article 3 became fully and automatically applicable to J&K. This gave Parliament the unrestricted authority to reorganise the state, just as it could with any other Indian state.

Chronological Breakdown of the Abrogation of Article 370

- STEP 1: J&K Under President's Rule (Since December 2018)

1. No elected Chief Minister or Legislative Assembly.
2. J&K was under President's Rule (Article 356).

3. The Governor acted as the State Government, under control of the Centre

- STEP 2: President Uses Article 370(1)(d)

1. This Article allows the President to apply parts of the Indian Constitution to J&K
2. But it needs concurrence of the State Government.
3. How was this done in 2019?
4. The word "State Government" was treated as meaning "Governor" (since no elected govt).
5. The Governor gave concurrence — on behalf of the Centre.

- STEP 3: President Issues Order C.O. 272 on 5 August 2019

1. This order made two big changes:
2. Applied the full Indian Constitution to J&K, removing special status.
3. Changed meanings of some key terms by modifying Article 367:

a. The term "Government of the State" was reinterpreted to mean the Governor of Jammu and Kashmir, who was then acting under President's Rule (since there was no elected state government or council of ministers).
b. The term "Sadr-i-Riyasat" (an earlier title used for the head of the state) was also redefined to mean the Governor.
c. Finally, the term "Constituent Assembly" (which had dissolved in 1957) was reinterpreted to mean the Legislative Assembly of Jammu and Kashmir.

d. These reinterpretations allowed the central government to move forward with the abrogation of Article 370, even though the original mechanisms (like the Constituent Assembly's recommendation) were no longer available.

- STEP 4: No Assembly? No Problem — Use Parliament!

As per convention under President's Rule: the Parliament of India acts like the Legislative Assembly of the state. So, when Article 370(3) said: "President needs recommendation of the Constituent Assembly…"It was now read as: "President needs recommendation of the Legislative Assembly…" and since there was no Assembly, Parliament filled that role.

- STEP 5: Rajya sabha Passes Resolution (5 August 2019)

Rajya Sabha passed a resolution recommending that Article 370 be abrogated (removed)

- STEP 5: Lok Sabha Approval (6 August 2019)

The Statutory Resolution recommending the abrogation of Article 370 under Article 370(3) was passed. This approval followed the Rajya Sabha's passage on 5 August, completing the parliamentary procedure required to allow the President to issue C.O. 273, which formally rendered Article 370 inoperative.

- STEP 6: President Issues C.O. 273 (6 August 2019)

1. Based on Parliament's recommendation,

2. President issued Constitution Order C.O. 273
3. Officially made Article 370 inoperative.

The Jammu and Kashmir Reorganisation Bill, 2019

Introduced alongside the second resolution, the Reorganisation Bill proposed:

- Bifurcation of the State: The State of Jammu and Kashmir would be split into two Union Territories:

1. Union Territory of Jammu and Kashmir (with a Legislative Assembly),
2. Union Territory of Ladarkh (without a Legislative Assembly, like Chandigarh).

- Governance Structure:

1. Jammu & Kashmir would have a Lieutenant Governor and a legislative assembly, but with limited powers, particularly in matters relating to public order and police (which remained under the Centre).
2. Ladakh would be governed by an Administrator appointed by the President, with no legislative body.

- High Court and Judiciary:

1. The existing J&K High Court would continue to function, now for the Union Territory of Jammu and Kashmir.

2. For Ladakh, judicial jurisdiction was extended through administrative arrangements.

- Legislative Representation:

1. Jammu and Kashmir retained 5 Lok Sabha seats, while Ladakh was given 1 Lok Sabha seat.
2. There was no representation for either UT in the Rajya Sabha until further constitutional or legislative changes were made.

- Applicability of Laws:

1. All central laws would be applicable to both UTs from the date of enactment.
2. Existing state laws were to be reviewed and repealed, amended, or retained as per future notifications.

With the Reorganisation Bill passed and the constitutional and legal framework of Jammu and Kashmir fundamentally recast, the Indian Union had entered an entirely new phase in its relationship with the region. What had once been a state marked by exceptional autonomy, defined by its own constitution and special status under Article 370, now stood reconstituted—legally, administratively, and politically—into Union Territories directly governed under the same constitutional framework as the rest of India.

The developments of 5 and 6 August 2019 did not merely represent a legislative maneuver or constitutional reinterpretation—they marked the culmination of a 70-year-long constitutional journey, and the defining turning point in India's federal and political landscape.

What began in 1947 as a negotiated accession under unique terms, crystallized in Article 370, gradually transformed through decades of Presidential Orders, political accords, and federal tension, before being finally dismantled through a carefully staged legal and parliamentary sequence.

By rendering Article 370 inoperative, Parliament did not just withdraw a special provision—it symbolically dissolved the wall of constitutional exceptionalism that had insulated Jammu and Kashmir from full integration. And through the Jammu and Kashmir Reorganisation Act, 2019, it redefined the region's political geography, effectively downgrading a state into Union Territories, something unprecedented in India's constitutional history.

CHAPTER TWO

CONCLUSION

The saga of Article 370, as unfolded in this book, is a profound reflection of India's relentless quest to reconcile unity with diversity, sovereignty with autonomy, and justice with power. Crafted in 1949 as a temporary provision to bridge Jammu and Kashmir's unique circumstances with India's constitutional framework, Article 370 symbolized a delicate compact—one tested by decades of political turbulence, militancy, and evolving federal dynamics. Its abrogation in 2019, executed through a masterful legal maneuver, marked a seismic, nation-defining moment, completing J&K's formal assimilation into India while igniting debates that resonate across political, judicial, and societal dimensions.

To some, this was the long-overdue fulfillment of national integration, rectifying an "interim provision" that had overstayed its purpose. To others, it represented the loss of constitutional federalism and democratic consent, altering a bilateral understanding without the people's direct mandate. But regardless of one's perspective, the transformation was legally comprehensive, procedurally executed, and politically irreversible. The repeal of Article 370 and the reorganization of J&K into two Union

Territories—Jammu and Kashmir with a legislature, and Ladakh under direct Central administration—have ushered in an era of legal uniformity, promising greater administrative efficiency, development parity, and the uniform application of laws. Yet, the people of Jammu and Kashmir faced the erosion of long-held constitutional guarantees without direct political representation at the moment of change, raising questions about the balance between central authority and regional identity.

The legacy of Article 370 endures not in its legal text but in the philosophical, legal, and political questions it leaves behind—questions that challenge India's vision as a pluralistic, federal democracy.

To the readers, I pose these mind-bending inquiries: Philosophically, can true unity thrive without embracing difference, or does the erasure of special provisions risk alienating the identities it seeks to integrate? Legally, was the abrogation a triumph of constitutional sovereignty or a circumvention of democratic consent, given the absence of an elected J&K assembly? Politically, can centralized governance heal decades of alienation, or does it deepen the chasm between state and citizen in a region scarred by mistrust? Will constitutional equality lead to emotional and political integration? Can the loss of autonomy be balanced by development, stability, and democratic restoration? How will this reshape the idea of federalism in India for other regions with special arrangements, such as those under Article 371?

What lies ahead for Jammu and Kashmir will depend not just on constitutional text but on how governance, development, justice, and civil liberties are shaped in the years to come. The true test lies in implementation, fairness, and inclusivity. The return to democratic elections, the restoration of statehood (as promised on the floor of Parliament), and a genuine reconciliation with local identity and aspirations will be critical to validating the changes made in 2019. The story of Article 370 has ended, but the story of Jammu and Kashmir within the Indian Union—as equal, yet historically distinct—continues to unfold.

J&K's constitutional journey mirrors India's democratic evolution: a balancing act between unity and diversity, sovereignty and autonomy, central authority and regional identity. The abrogation of Article 370 may have closed a chapter, but it has opened a new one—one that will be written not just in statutes and courtrooms but in the everyday lives and futures of millions in the region. Only time—and history—will determine whether this bold legal reengineering becomes a foundation for unity and progress or a precedent fraught with complexity and contestation. As J&K navigates this new era, the narrative of Article 370 remains a testament to India's audacious federal experiment, urging continued dialogue, empathy, and reconciliation to forge a future of lasting peace and

Matters Related To Review/ correction Of The Contents Of The Book

Dear Readers,

As you engage with this book, which chronicles the intricate historical, political, and constitutional journey of Article 370 and Jammu and Kashmir, I wish to share a note about its creation and purpose. This work aims to illuminate a pivotal chapter in India's history—from the critical accession of 1947 to the transformative abrogation of Article 370 in 2019. It is a story of unity and diversity, sovereignty and autonomy, and the ongoing quest for reconciliation.

Every word has been chosen with care, grounded in rigorous fact-checking and informed by credible sources. However, as with any human endeavor, errors may inadvertently occur in such a multifaceted narrative. Historical and legal accounts are subject to interpretation, and new evidence or perspectives may surface. My commitment is to provide a reliable and thought-provoking resource, and your engagement is essential to that mission.

If you identify any factual oversight, wish to suggest improvements, or want to share your thoughts, I warmly invite you to contact me at 19subhranil@gmail.com. Your feedback—whether a correction, a review, or a reflection—will be greatly appreciated and will enrich the ongoing dialogue about J&K's past, present, and future. Your insights are invaluable in refining our understanding of this intricate subject.

This book is more than a historical recounting; it is an invitation to wrestle with profound questions about federalism, identity, and justice in India. I hope it sparks curiosity and inspires meaningful conversations as you explore the legacy of Article 370 and the evolving story of Jammu and Kashmir within the Indian Union. Thank you for your readership and for being part of this journey.

Sincerely,

Subhranil Bhowmik